JOURNAL COLLECTION
YEARS 2000 TO 2005

More Ideas About Parenting with Less Stress

Jim Fay, Charles Fay
& Foster W. Clin

Love and Logic
INSTITUTE, Inc.

The Love and Logic Institute, Inc.
2207 Jackson Street
Golden, Colorado 80401-2300
www.loveandlogic.com

Institute For Professional Development, Ltd. d.b.a. The Love and Logic Institute, Inc.
2207 Jackson Street, Golden, CO 80401-2300
www.loveandlogic.com
800-338-4065

Library of Congress Cataloging-in-Publication Data

Fay, Jim.
  More ideas about parenting with less stress : love and logic journal collection years 2000 to 2005 / Jim Fay, Charles Fay, and Foster W. Cline.
    p. cm.
  Includes bibliographical references and index.
  1. Child rearing. 2. Parenting. 3. Parent and child. I. Fay, Charles, 1964- II. Cline, Foster. III. Love and logic journal. IV. Title.
HQ769.M683 2005
649'.1--dc22

                              2005018952

Project Coordinator: Carol Thomas
Editing by Jason Cook, Denver, CO
Indexing by Douglas J. Easton, New West Indexing, Westminster, CO
Cover and interior design by Michael Snell
    Shade of the Cottonwood, Topeka, KS

Published and Printed in the United States of America

CONTENTS

About the Authors.. vi
Introduction.. ix

Volume 16.. 1
   It's Never Too Late.. 3
   When It's Time for Potty Training 5
   Easing Peer Pressure with Love and Logic 8
   A FOSTER CLINE Q & A SESSION 10
   CLINE'S CORNER ♦ Alternatives to Saying No:
      All About Not Saying No to Your Kids 15
   Love and Logic Position Paper on the Use of
      Spanking as a Disciplinary Tool 18
   Don't Let Pets Bear the Consequences 19
   Survival Skills for the Real World....................... 22
   Using Love and Logic Through the Years 24
   CLINE'S CORNER ♦ Help Your Child to Share 25
   A FOSTER CLINE Q & A SESSION 27
   Poor Decisions More Costly for Today's Teens—Survey...... 29
   A Spoiled Brat in Training.................................. 30
   Love and Logic Treats Both Symptoms and Causes............ 34
   CLINE'S CORNER ♦ The Art of Micro Love and Logic.......... 38
   A FOSTER CLINE Q & A SESSION 41
   What Do You Value?.. 41
   A Little Boredom Is a Good Thing 45
   CLINE'S CORNER ♦ Building Character and
      Discipline in Children.................................... 50

Volume 17.. 55
   If Kids Can Hear Promises, They Can Hear Requests 57
   Positive Relationships: Reaching Tough Students 59
   CLINE'S CORNER ♦ "The School Just Isn't Being Fair" 63
   What an Inconvenience 66

Solving the Dependent Learner Problem:
  Mornings May Be More Important Than You Think!...... 68
CLINE'S CORNER ♦ "What Shall We Do with This Teen?" 74
"Is That You, Grandma?" 78
Toxic Birthday Parties: Just Say "No!" to
  Keeping Up with the Joneses 82
Helping Kids Cope with Tragedy: What to
  Say to Help Them Feel Safe and Secure 85
CLINE'S CORNER ♦ Keep Your Options Open:
  Don't Give Warnings.. 87
"Boy, Did I Learn My Lesson" 89
Getting Kids Up in the Morning.. 93

Volume 18... 95
  How Do You Know When They're Ready? 97
  Easygoing Kids Need Love and Logic Too! 99
  Understanding Kids Who Hate School 103
  Depressed Teens Don't Have to Feel So Bad!.................... 108
  When Is Stepping In, Helping Out, and
    Rescuing Warranted?.. 113
  How to Raise a Trophy Kid 116
  When's It Time for Kids to Make Their Own Choices? 119
  The Evolution of the Helicopter Parent:
    The Turbo-Attack Helicopter Model 121
  When Parents Have Different Parenting Styles:
    Believe It or Not ... Kids Can Handle It! 125
  Follies of Youth—Our Own and Our Kids' 129

Volume 19... 133
  A Happy Person vs. a Good Person.................................... 135
  Honesty Deficit Disorder (HDD) ... or,
    What to Do When Your Kids Lie 139
  Creativity in Children... 143
  Broken Agreements 146

"Big Boys Do It in the Potty" ... and Other
   Adventures: How to Get Your Toddler to Do
   Just About Anything You Want 150
Love and Logic Also Works on Our Elderly Parents 155
If You Can, They Can: Learning to Handle
   Life's Bumps and Bruises 158
Love and Logic Thoughts on Therapy 162
"I Just Want My Kids to Be Happy" 165
Give Your Kids the Gift of Wise Money
   Management: Raise Kids Who'll Grow
   Up to Miss *You* ... Rather Than Your Money 169
Consequences with *Pizzazz* 173

Volume 20 177
   Computer Game Addiction 179
   Stickers, Tokens, Points, and Pizza Parties:
      Some Thoughts on the Use of Tangible Rewards 182
   The Road to Wisdom Is Paved with Mistakes 189
   The Impact of Anxiety on Academic Achievement:
      Why Too Many Kids Are Learning Far Too Little 192
   Five Gifts for Your Children 198
   Picking Fights and Losing Battles 200
   The Problem with Entitlement 205
   The Highs and Lows of Entitlement 208
   Marriage: Love and Logic Isn't Just for Kids 212

Index 217

JIM FAY

The legendary Jim Fay began his career as a teacher and for over three decades served in public, private, and parochial schools. He spent seventeen years as a school principal and administrator, and for nearly thirty years has been a public speaker. Jim has served as a national and international educational consultant to schools, parent organizations, counselors, mental health organizations, and the U.S. military.

Jim believes his major accomplishment in life is the development of a unique philosophy of practical techniques for enhancing communication between children and adults, known as Love and Logic. Jim has taken complex problems and broken them down into simple, easy-to-use concepts and techniques that can be understood and used by anyone. Hundreds of thousands of people have expressed how Love and Logic has enhanced their relationships with their children.

Jim is one of America's most sought after presenters in the area of parenting and school discipline. His practical techniques are revolutionizing the way parents and professionals deal with children to help them become responsible, thinking people and enhance their own self-concept.

CHARLES FAY, PH.D.

Charles Fay, Ph.D., is a parent, school psychologist, author, and consultant to schools, parent groups, and mental health professionals across the United States. His expertise in developing and teaching practical discipline strategies has been refined through work with severely disturbed youth in school, hospital, and community settings. Charles has assisted many thousands of parents and teachers in learning practical and powerful techniques to gain control of their homes and classrooms, maintaining loving relationships with their children, and preparing children to become responsible and caring adults. His book *Love and Logic Magic for Early Childhood: Practical Parenting from Birth to Six Years* has obtained bestseller status. Charles frequently comments, "After all of these years, I still love being around my dad!"

FOSTER W. CLINE, M.D.

Dr. Cline is a nationally recognized psychiatrist and cofounder of the Cline/Fay Institute, Inc. He is a favorite consultant to psychiatric institutes, schools, and parent groups. His writings are the source of many revolutionary approaches to dealing with childhood problems. He has written several books, including *Uncontrollable Kids: From Heartbreak to Hope* and, coauthoring with Jim Fay, *Parenting with Love and Logic, Parenting Teens with Love and Logic,* and *Grandparenting with Love and Logic.*

Foster is known for his ability to provide creative, effective solutions for behavior problems. His presentations are lively and humorous, while providing practical techniques that produce immediate results. Foster has an uncanny ability to share his ideas and expertise in such a way that readers and audiences immediately envision themselves being more successful with young people.

The Love and Logic quarterly newsletter, known as the *Love and Logic Journal*, was first published in 1984. It was with considerable trepidation that I agreed to write the articles for the first year. I remember saying, "Once we start this, Foster and I will be obligated to come up with new topics and articles each year. I'm going to run out of material and knowledge in a short time. I can't imagine being productive and creative for more than just a few years."

What do you know? That was twenty-one years ago. The world of parenting, teaching, and childhood has continued to evolve along with all the associated new challenges and topics for articles. My worst fears didn't come true after all. Each year, people ask us for more creative solutions to new and different dilemmas.

During its first ten years the Love and Logic Institute was deluged with requests for reprints of *Journal* articles. The obvious solution to this was to publish a collection of all the articles that appeared in the *Journal*. That book was titled the *Tenth Anniversary Journal Collection*. Now that I think back on it, the title was less than creative. However, parents and teachers found great value in keeping this collection of articles close at hand as a resource for times when they experienced problems with their kids.

Ten years ago, my son, Dr. Charles Fay, joined our organization. Being a gifted writer, he contributed to the *Journal* on a regular basis, the result being that now—after another ten years—the number of articles has grown considerably larger. Because even a selection of these articles won't fit into one book, we're offering this new collection in two volumes, *Taking the Stress Out of Raising Great Kids* (years 1995 to 2000) and *More Ideas About Parenting with Less Stress* (years 2000 to 2005).

As with the first, tenth-anniversary collection, these articles are best read randomly, one at a time, as the need arises. Keep your collection in a handy place, such as on the night stand or in the bathroom, and don't be afraid to let your kids read the articles if they become curious about the development of your new skills.

The wonderful thing about Love and Logic is that even if your kids know what you are going to do, they can't stop you from doing what is right.

I hope you find this two-volume collection helpful and entertaining. Foster, Charles, and I are proud to offer our view of the world of raising and developing responsible kids who are endowed with the character to become our future leaders.

Read and enjoy,
Jim Fay, President, Love and Logic Institute, Inc.

VOLUME

16

It's Never Too Late
By Jim Fay
Vol. 16, No. 1

"It won't work with a sixteen-year-old!" Then I heard it again. Every time I made a suggestion to the audience, I heard it. "It won't work with a sixteen-year-old."

The source of this negativity was a woman in the back row. She would turn to the person next to her, using a stage whisper that everyone could hear. The rest of the audience was becoming so disturbed by her behavior that I found a need to stop the presentation and deal with her.

"What's the problem?" I inquired.

"These ideas might work with little kids," she insisted, "but my kid is sixteen years old and they would never work on him."

"That might be," I suggested. "Would you be willing to prove that to the group?"

"What does that mean?"

"Well, I guess it means that you learn the skills here tonight, experiment with them tomorrow, and report back to the group tomorrow night with the results."

This turned her on. "I know they won't work. Nothing works on this kid. I don't have to experiment to know that he'll just ignore me like he always does."

For some reason our short discussion settled her down so she could listen to the rest of the presentation about the power of giving kids choices instead of demands.

Our group got a big surprise the next day when she returned to class.

"I need to make an announcement," she blurted out. "This stuff works on sixteen-year-olds. I can't believe it! Last night I was determined to prove that choices don't work with a tough kid like mine—I was just waiting for my chance.

"Chuck was going out the door without his coat. Ordinarily I have a big argument with him about wearing a coat and he ends up telling me to get out of his face and mind my own business. As he walked past me, I said, 'Hey, Chuck.'

"He muttered, 'Uh?'"

"I hit him with, 'Are you wearing a coat tonight or just carrying it?'"

"Still muttering to himself, he said, 'Uh, I don't know. Guess I'm carrying it.' He walked out of the house with his coat in his hand, not even realizing what had happened to him."

This was a great moment for the entire class. We had a chance to discuss whether it is ever too late to start using the Love and Logic techniques. As the discussion went on, the members of the class started to realize that Love and Logic is not designed to change kids, even though that is the final result.

Love and Logic changes the way adults talk to a youngster, automatically changing the child's reciprocal response.

Picture in your mind the typical response of a kid upon hearing an adult demanding, "Don't you talk to me like that!" The picture that comes to mind is that of an angry response from the child.

Now, picture the same kid hearing the adult saying, "I'll be glad to listen when your voice sounds like mine." A totally different picture comes to your mind.

How does a typical teen react to a parent who says, "Don't be begging for more money. You wasted your allowance and now you're just going to have to go without. I don't care if you have a date. You waste ever penny I give you. I'm sick and tired of bailing you out every week!"?

This youngster will probably start arguing about not getting enough money in the first place. He will no doubt tell his father that the other kids in the neighborhood have loving parents who provide allowances that are adequate so their kids don't have to come begging each week.

I bet you can picture many parents who, at this point, give in. "Oh, all right! Take it! But this is the last time. I mean it!" Would you agree that the parent is now angry and frustrated while the kid is satisfied?

What if this dad discovers Love and Logic and comes up with a different response next week? What do you suppose will be the teen's reaction when Dad says, "What a bummer. Well, not to worry, I'll be giving out allowances on Saturday as usual. Come see me then."

We can expect this teen to argue that he needs the money now. This will give Dad a chance to use his new Love and Logic one-liner: "I know, and I love you too much to argue."

How long will it be before we see a frustrated teenager and a satisfied parent if Dad is willing to stick to his new Love and Logic one-liner, regardless of what his child says? Has there been a dramatic shift in the balance of power in this family?

Does the age of the child determine whether Love and Logic works, or is it the willingness of the parent to change that is the important factor?

What is my suggestion for people who question if it is ever too late to start using Love and Logic? Learn the techniques. Wait for an opportune moment, and experiment. That is the only way you will know for sure.

By the way, Love and Logic works on adults. The subject of one of my next articles will be how Shirley, my wife, trained me to listen very carefully when she says the words, "Jim, would it be reasonable ... ?"

© 2000 Jim Fay

When It's Time for Potty Training
By Charles Fay, Ph.D.
Vol. 16, No. 1

There are so many wonderful ways to help our kids think for themselves and make them wiser. The following is a story about Harry, who learned, along with his family, that potty training can be fun, for both parent and child. Take a look at how Harry and his dad had a great time.

Harry Trains for the Super Bowl

Little Harry lives in a house that has two bathrooms—one upstairs and one downstairs. One morning, his father says, "Hey, Harry! You want to use the upstairs potty or the downstairs potty?"

"Upstairs! Upstairs potty!" says Harry.

A Love and Logic parent, his father says, "You want to have fun while we're doing this, or not have fun?"

The great thing about choices with little kids is that they love making them—the more foolish, the better. The decisions they make on their own make them feel important; plus, the process contributes to bonding. Furthermore, the more choices parents give, the more kids have to think.

Harry looks at his dad as if he were crazy, and giggles, "Fun! I want to have fun!"

"Great," says his dad. "Do you want to bring a drink in with you, or do you want to wait until you're done?"

"Wait till I'm done!"

His dad gives Harry lots of little choices surrounding this activity of potty training. "Do you want to bring Clarence, your stuffed sea otter, with us, or do you want to leave him?"

"Bring him!" Harry says, as he goes to retrieve his favorite stuffed playmate.

Now Harry's dad moves to the next step—modeling. Although some parents might find it a little embarrassing, modeling is the best way to teach your kids just about anything. Harry's dad thinks it's great.

"Hey! I really have to use the bathroom!" he says enthusiastically to his son. "Why don't you come in with me? Let's go play. This is how it's done!"

He shows his son how he uses the bathroom. "This is so much fun!" he laughs. "Someday when you're big enough, I bet you'll be able to use the potty like me! Then you can have fun too! Boy! I love using the potty! I can even wipe myself! Check this out!" He flushes the toilet and waves "Bye-bye!" as he looks into it.

The logic here is clear. Kids want to be like their parents. Whatever parents do, kids naturally want to be able to do, too. And if parents think it's fun, kids will too. So, parents have a choice when it comes to potty training:

- We can allow ourselves to become embarrassed and refuse to model.
- We can fight with our kids over the issue, and try to force them to be ready before they actually are.
- We can say, "Let's have fun! Let's take the pain out of this process, and enjoy ourselves! I'm going to demonstrate how much fun this is, and then, when you're ready, you'll think it's fun, too!"

When Accidents Happen

If you know how to ride a bike, you probably remember falling a few times before finding the right balance. When we're learning something new, accidents are bound to happen. So it is with our children when they are at potty-training age.

Successful parents dole out empathy and say, "Oh, you had an accident! That's too bad! I love you, Sweetie." They take their time, and don't rush anything, because there's no set timetable for potty training. Every child has his or her own schedule of development.

Some children potty-train at two, some when they're four, and some at every age in between. It all depends on the child. A wise parent locks in the empathy and waits for the kids to develop the skill on their own. Then, when a child is successful, a parent can say, "You did it! Good for you!"

Unsuccessful parents have a pattern, too. When their kids make a mistake, they get upset or angry. They say, "You messed your pants again! That's not nice! We don't do that! Now you better learn how to do this right! You're going to sit here until you use the potty!"

You can guess what happens. The child sees frustrated parents, and the child gets frustrated, too. Like any task we're expected to perform under pressure, potty training becomes an undesirable chore.

There's a psychological theory that says that people potty-trained in this way grow up to be "anal-retentive." Since it's not a Love and Logic theory, we'll leave that decision up to you.

© 2000 Charles Fay, Ph.D.

Easing Peer Pressure with Love and Logic
By Charles Fay, Ph.D.
Vol. 16, No. 1

What's a parent to do or say when the kids start "hanging out" with friends who remind them more of the late-night horror show than the sweet little pals everyone hopes their children will choose?

Peer pressure is stronger than ever, and many kids are faced with life-or-death decisions about drugs, alcohol, sex, and violence starting as early as elementary school!

Out of great love for their children, some parents take the "bulldozer" approach to this problem. They rev up their engines, make a lot of noise and smoke, and try to overpower their kids: "You stay away from that Tommy! He's bad news! He's going to get you in a world of trouble!"

Every time parents give this type of lecture, they imply that their child is a wimp! "You are so weak you can't choose good friends and think for yourself when they want you to do something that's wrong," is the underlying message sent by this approach.

Sadly, the parent–child relationship is wounded, and the child now is forced to make poor decisions to "win" the battle.

Other parents take a completely different tack. These parents try to show their love by staying away from sensitive issues such as peer pressure, drugs, alcohol, violence, and sex. "Kid, I don't care enough about you to be involved in your life," is the unintentional yet very powerful message sent by this strategy.

What's a loving parent to do? At the Love and Logic Institute, we give parents practical ideas for staying involved in our children's lives and teaching responsibility, without creating power struggles and hurt feelings! Listed below are some of these ideas:

1. Love and Logic parents know that the fastest way to get kids to spend more time with friends we don't like is to forbid them from doing so!

2. Love and Logic parents send "You are strong" messages ("Your friends are lucky to have someone like you who can show them how to make smart choices.") instead of "You are weak" messages ("Stay away from that Billy-Sue. She's trouble!").

3. Love and Logic parents help their kids take the pressure out of saying no by giving them permission to say, "No way. Last time I did that my parents really let me have it."

4. Love and Logic parents encourage responsibility by saying, "We know you are the kind of kid who is strong enough to live with the consequences of your choices."

5. Love and Logic parents send plenty of unconditional "I love you" messages. They also show their kids how much they care by asking them who they are going to be with and where they are going.

Writing a letter to your child about peer pressure is an excellent way to "get the ball rolling" in a healthy way. Here's an example written by two Love and Logic parents:

Dear Collin,

We love you so much! Sometimes smart kids like you find out their friends aren't making such smart decisions about drugs, alcohol, sex, or other serious things. At those times, friends are really lucky to have someone like you who can show them how to make good decisions.

Sometimes even really smart kids like you feel pressured to do things they think are wrong or dangerous just to keep their friends. They worry that other kids will think they are wimps if they don't go along.

If you think it might help, try saying something like, "No way. Last time I did something like that, I got caught and my parents almost killed me."

The good thing about having friends that make poor decisions is that it gives you lots of practice making good ones! We only ask one thing of you. Before you leave us to spend time with your friends, give us a hug and leave us a list of names and phone numbers.

We promise never to call these numbers and snoop on you unless we start to worry because you haven't come home on time. If you are running late, please give us a call so we don't worry too much.

If you ever do make a poor decision, we won't yell, lecture, or stop loving you. We will probably feel very sad for you, but we both know you are the kind of kid who can live with the consequences of your choices.

Your friends really are lucky to have you. We are, too!

Love,
Mom and Dad

© *2000 Charles Fay, Ph.D.*

A Foster Cline Q & A Session

VOL. 16, NO. 1

Question

How social should middle school children be and how important are friends? My middle school son is in a world of his own. He is shy but intelligent. He does not really fit in with the other children. On the surface he seems fine, but I am bothered by the fact that he has no close friends.

His time is taken up with reading (at a very advanced reading level) and being alone. He makes "jokes" around his peers that are over their level of thinking. He is not understood by his peers, does not try to belong, and seems content that way. But as a mother I see the sadness underneath. What can I do short of counseling?

—Concerned

Answer

Many great kids in middle school are in a world of their own. Often they are very shy and bright. But take heart! If you lived every day in a junior high or middle school, you might want to be in a world of your own, too.

It is not every adult that happily and quickly volunteers to teach Sunday School to the junior high schoolers—especially if they are bright! (Just kidding—sorta!)

And your son might be right about being ahead of the other kids in thinking. If he can easily abstract metaphors—"Still waters run deep" and "Every rose has its thorns"—he has moved into "Formal Operations" in his thinking, and left all the little "Concrete Operations" thinkers behind. Piaget wrote about this essential step toward adult thinking that takes place as kids become teens.

So often in my private practice, one hour I would see a mom who was rightly worried about what group her junior high kid was running with and how influenced by the peer group he was.

The next hour I would see the mom of the kid who no longer ran with the same group of kids and she was worried about her kid isolating from the group. And I would think to myself, "Oh, concerned mom, quit complaining and thank your lucky stars!"

Seriously, many of the loners in junior high and middle school grow up to be the great independent thinkers and leaders. They often find their niche and appropriate group of friends in high school, when differences are celebrated and unique gifts are recognized.

Now, if your kid is isolating himself, has few friends, has dark posters on the wall, listens to heavy metal, and is not very fun or responsive to you ... then that is an entirely different matter and counseling should be sought.

More likely, your son may be reflecting worry or disappointment about his not having a lot of friends. Rather than show him those emotions, celebrate with him his unique qualities and interests, and if you and your hubby have a good relationship with him and are friends with him, I'll guarantee he'll have friends in the future!

• • •

Question

How important are newborn schedules? Do you believe in keeping babies on a schedule? I have read many books and they seem to say a four-hour schedule is correct, even if it means waking the baby during the daytime.

Personally, it seems to me to make sense to let the child make the schedule during the day. Of course, I want my baby to sleep at night, the customary hours.

—Confused

Answer

I'm not a big believer in tight schedules for newborns. I think the mother needs to fit to the infant's rhythm. Then as the child grows older, the rhythm becomes a hymn that both sing, and the child starts molding to more normal sleeping hours naturally. If a child is overly fussy or difficult, rocking, singing, and patting definitely help.

The rule for the first five months of life is that you do everything possible to soothe the baby. As the weeks pass, it is gratifying to bring the baby into the parents' bed and allow him or her to sleep there. But that should *always* be because *you* want the company, not because they demand it or refuse to sleep without it.

Certainly a newborn needs frequent day and evening feedings, but I would be slow to wake up a child to feed them, particularly in the morning. Let them sleep. An evening feeding will help the infant sleep through the night. But a common mistake is attempting to keep the child up to all hours so he or she will sleep through the rest of the night.

There is a "magic moment" when most small infants roll their eyes around and they are obviously tired and about to lose it. *This* is the time to put them down, not waiting for that magic moment to pass, for fussiness to set in and crib unhappiness to continue. Infants sleep longer and better when put down in the "magic moment."

• • •

Question

How much television is appropriate? My eleven-year-old child wants a television in her room, but I am scared half to death about the type of shows on television. What are your thoughts on television in their bedroom and in general for children?

— Worried by TV

Answer

I have written a lot about TV. The main problem is when little kids, two through six years of age, watch TV and "good children's programming and videos" and don't learn *task* development and *task* focus.

I am sure this has led to a whole generation of kids who can't focus on tasks, fragment, and are misdiagnosed "ADD." (They have no trouble at all watching TV and *all TV requires is attention*. Most kids diagnosed with ADD are put in front of a TV or computer screen to settle them down!)

But that is not your question directly. If I have a great eleven-year-old, who is responsible and clear-headed, I don't worry too much about content. But I do let children know that every moment sitting in front of the boob tube is a moment lost from life—a moment when they have not accomplished a darn thing.

I tell children how many adults now use their free time to watch something rather than *do* something and that I hope that this doesn't happen to them.

Television is addicting. Therefore I encourage and celebrate children setting their own limits, as television is about the most benign addiction possible as they learn to control addictions.

If the child absolutely cannot set his or her own reasonable limits, I'm willing to, but I don't like it! (And I let the child know I don't like it, and am a little disappointed in him or her.)

When I see TV in bedrooms I feel bad for both the adults and the kids. Games, conversation, and reading individually or to each other are better ideas.

TV in America halts both conversation and creative thinking. Overall, when any adult or child spends more of his or her free time watching something than doing something, it is a sad day!

• • •

Question

Do you believe child harnesses are suitable for toddlers? My grand-mother used a harness for me when I was young on shopping trips. That seemed to make her feel comfortable and I do not seem to have suffered any lasting effects.

With places so busy these days at malls and out in public, I thought it would be beneficial as a mother of three small children. Some of my friends think they are horrible; I am thinking more along the lines of safety.

—Mom

Answer

I'm not a big believer in harnesses. If you have a number of kids, I can understand how the idea would be pretty appealing! And you certainly aren't going to ruin a child by use of the harness in and of itself. However, there is a drawback to using a harness. It clearly says to toddlers that the only way they can be expected to stay in contact with Mom is by external control.

A mother who expects her toddler to stay with her, and a mother who believes that the only way to really keep track of the toddler is with a harness, may have very different expectations and these expectations often are communicated to the child.

That is the interesting issue. All moms have to examine their own expectations if a harness is used. Is it because they are very controlling or overly concerned about the child getting lost, kid-napped, or killed, or is it simply a momentary convenience during a very short period of toddlerhood when a bundle of kids need to be kept track of?

Remember, as long as children are in a harness, you are right, their safety is ensured. *But* sometimes the kids are *out* of the harness and must learn to watch out for cars, to hold Mommy's hand when crossing roads, etc.

I come down on the side of believing that when a child is old enough to walk, he or she is plenty old enough to learn and respond to "Basic German Shepherd"—"Come, sit, go, no, stay, heel, hold my hand."

© 2000 Foster W. Cline, M.D.

CLINE'S CORNER

Alternatives to Saying No:
All About Not Saying No to Your Kids
By Foster W. Cline, M.D.

VOL. 16, NO. 1

There are alternatives to saying no. I can just hear all you dear readers immediately saying, "Alternatives to saying no? What is Foster Cline talking about? That is the whole problem with today's youth. No one tells them no. They need to be told no a lot more!"

This is not necessarily true. Practically every juvenile delinquent I have ever worked with had parents who said no. They said no to their child's drug use, and they said no to larceny, disrespect, and dropping out of school.

No parent wants to raise a delinquent! All these kids were told no. Indeed, the whole country has been told to "just say no." But telling the country to just say no is not working very well, is it? Drugs are still big business.

Professionally, it would appear to me that the whole problem for ineffective parents lies not in their saying no too infrequently, but in saying it too often and *not meaning it enough!*

There are two general areas in which parents say no. The first area involves possession, as in, "No, you can't have it." We can dispense with this area pretty quickly with a cookbook technique.

Parents hardly ever have to say no to what their child wants. It is best to say yes, as in, "Yes, Honey, if anyone ever needed that (whatever it is that the child wants), it is you ... so buy it." To which the average kid replies, "I don't have enough *money*." To which the average parent best responds, "Well, what a bummer, then I guess even though you want it, you won't have it! Pretty upsetting, huh?"

The second area of parental no involves children's actions, as in, "No, you can't do it." The beauty of saying, "No, you can't do it," is that the statement is almost always enforceable for little kids, who almost always obey anyway. The problem is that "No, you can't do it" may not cut a lot of ice with teens. So it is better for all you parents to get in the habit of practicing some other technique when your child is small.

While saying no does have some advantages in childhood—it is quick, it is easy, and it is almost always obeyed—it does have some distinct disadvantages:

- It implies that the child wouldn't say no to him- or herself.
- It may invite rebellion.
- It may cause resentment.
- With teens, it may be outright disobeyed.
- Once parents say no they may be painting themselves into a corner.
- It says that parental judgment is better than the child's own judgment of the situation.
- It may imply that the child is incapable of making good choices.

There is one great advantage to saying no. As parents, we can always say it! Since it is always an option, let's not rush into it! Let's try other things first.

There are many, many alternatives to saying no that have fewer disadvantages. Older infants and toddlers can be distracted: "Oh, you want to grab at that glass, well look at these keys."

After early toddlerhood, however, distraction won't work again until preteen girls have horses! Of course, that is an expensive distraction, and not all parents can afford a creature that always idles, constantly pollutes, and has no off switch.

Teens and older kids aren't so easily distracted; however, there are other alternatives to no. The four primary alternatives to saying no are "I" messages, consequences, choices, and saying yes.

Let's look at a typical no that parents might give an elementary-age child: "No, you can't go skiing, because you didn't finish your chores."

- Give an "I" message: "I'm happier when I'm skiing with people who pull their share of the load around here."
- Outline a consequence: "If you finish your work, the next time we go it will be so good to have you with us."
- Give a choice: "You have a choice of doing the work before we go skiing or completing it when we are skiing."

The rules of thumb for if and when to say no to an adolescent are:

- If the youth is incapable of saying no to him- or herself.
- If there is a solid danger that life, limb, or future happiness could be at stake.
- If no will be obeyed or if the failure to obey can be consequenced effectively. (This very simple fact is ignored by a lot of parents who make the situation worse by saying no to a child who won't obey.)
- If the situation is such that the parent cannot handle the risk— however slight it may be. (However, this is a dangerous area to get into with an adolescent.)

And let's look at alternatives to no with a teen. A parent might say, "You are *not* going to that party. No. I forbid it."

- Give an "I" message: "Honey, I don't feel very good about you going to that party, because I am concerned about the behavior of some of those kids."

- Outline a consequence: "Honey, if you do decide to go to that party, and the cops are called, do you know a good lawyer? Are you comfortable with the food in the county detention center?"
- Give a choice: "You have a choice of living in the home and following my rules, or living on your own, paying your own way, and living by your rules."
- Say yes: This is a rather simple solution, as the *most* common reason for adolescent rebellion occurs when parents say no too frequently to a basically responsible offspring.

If a parent doesn't know for sure whether to say no or yes, the rule of thumb is to say yes to a responsible child, and no to an irresponsible child if the no will be obeyed or can be consequenced effectively. Otherwise the parent simply has to rely on natural consequences teaching the lesson.

Looking back on my parenting years, I have realized that when my own responsible children were mightily hacked off at my saying no, it was an issue where I could have, and probably should have, said yes.

© 2000 Foster W. Cline, M.D.

Love and Logic Position Paper on the Use of Spanking as a Disciplinary Tool
By Jim Fay
VOL. 16, NO. 1

The previous position we outlined on spanking in the book *Parenting with Love and Logic,* unfortunately, was our thinking as of 1990, when the book was written. Since then our knowledge has grown. The world we live in has changed, and we have developed new techniques that are far more effective than spanking.

For the record, our present stance on spanking is:

1. There is no need for spanking.
2. Spanking is counterproductive. It makes the adult into the "bad guy" instead of the bad decision becoming the culprit.

3. Love and Logic techniques are far more powerful than spanking.
4. Most kids would much rather have a spanking than have their parents use Love and Logic techniques such as delaying the consequence while the parent thinks over the problem, develops a clear head, and then locks in the empathy before telling the child what the consequence will be.
5. Since we now have such better techniques, why even consider, or waste our time with, spanking?
6. A considerable amount of solid research is now available indicating the harmful, counterproductive results of using spanking as a disciplinary tool.

These six points plus others would make up the content of the chapter on spanking if we could write the book again, or when Pinion Press decides to update the book.

Please feel free to reproduce this article and provide it to others who happen to be interested in the Love and Logic position on spanking.

Sincerely,
Jim Fay
Chairman of the Board
Cline/Fay Institute, Inc.

© 2000 Jim Fay

Don't Let Pets Bear the Consequences
By Jim Fay
VOL. 16, No. 2

We got a puppy for our kids so they could learn some responsibility, but they soon tired of feeding and caring for him. Now he's always going hungry. Kids just don't want to be responsible nowadays. Now it's just one more thing for us to fight over. I guess we're going to have to find a new home for the dog.

How many times have you heard this from a frustrated parent? This kind of family situation is often brought about by a common misconception that taking care of animals is a good way of teaching kids to be responsible. I used to agree with this, but I no longer subscribe to this line of thinking.

Who experiences the consequence when little Hope forgets to feed Fluffy—Hope or her pet kitty? That's obvious, it's Fluffy. How sad for Fluffy. Who should be experiencing the consequence of Hope's careless act? Hope, not Fluffy.

Love and Logic teaches us that kids learn best through choices and consequences. They seldom learn from watching others live with consequences. They don't learn from lectures about how their actions affect others. It's important to give kids responsibilities with consequences that affect the kids directly.

Juan, our loving Chihuahua, taught me one of life's important lessons: Animals should not be used as objects to teach kids responsibility. Juan is faithful, sensitive to our emotions, and very attached to the people in our family. Animal science teaches us that Juan experiences many of the same kinds of emotions as people. For example, we watched him suffer depression, loss, and grief when his friend, the stray cat, left for good.

Watching Juan experience grief over the loss of his friend reminded us that many pets who become lovingly attached to families are carted off to animal shelters when the initial interest wears off. They languish in pens, suffering grief, loss, and confusion.

Steele, our German shepherd, caused Shirley and me to start thinking about the attachment animals develop for other animals, as well as the people they live with. Steele's best friend was Cheddar, our big orange cat. They slept together for years.

One sad day, Cheddar ran under the wheels of a car. The accident happened about a quarter of a mile down the road. Steele witnessed the death of his good friend. He ran to our house, throwing his body against the window until Shirley went out to see what was happening.

Steele insistently took Shirley's hand, almost dragging her to the scene of the accident. It was obvious that he was terribly upset.

Steele was never the same after that day. Later, as we learned more about animals, we realized what had happened. Steele went into a deep depression and, day-by-day, mourned himself to death.

Shirley and I often visit our local animal shelter. Our hearts ache as we see animals that have the same depressed look we saw on Steele's face. Many of these animals started out as happy pets in families who eventually tired of the responsibilities. They bonded with the family members and were abandoned to the animal shelter for reasons the animal will never understand.

I don't know anybody who would threaten a child with, "If you aren't responsible, I'm going to punish someone else." However, this is exactly what happens when kids don't feed or care for the pet. The youngster makes the mistake, and the animal experiences the consequence.

Pets are a great addition to the family, and can be a good source of learning for children when parents establish rules and expectations in advance. However, I am not referring to threats about the animal going away if it is not cared for.

The ideal situation for bringing a pet into the family is best described in the following family scenario. This wise parent sets up conditions under which the kids have some training in the care and feeding of their new pet.

The family has discussed the long-term responsibilities of taking an animal into the home. The parents also have decided, in advance, that they ultimately will take over the responsibilities if the kids prove unable or unwilling to handle the responsibilities:

PARENT: "Well, kids, Fluffy will not be able to feed and care for herself. You've told me that you will do that for her. This is a big responsibility. What do you think I will do if I see her not being fed on time?"

KIDS: "You'll take her back to the kennel?"

PARENT: "Of course not. That would be a very hurtful thing to do to an animal that loves us. I'll feed her. The most important thing is that she doesn't go hungry."

KIDS: "Are you going to get mad at us then?"

PARENT: "Of course not. I'll be glad to take over the job of caring for Fluffy. And it won't be a problem because you can take over some of my jobs. It'll all even out if you take over some of the jobs I don't like. That way, you'll be doing the jobs I don't like and Fluffy will be fed and happy. I think we'll all be a lot happier that way."

© 2000 Jim Fay

Survival Skills for the Real World
By Charles Fay, Ph.D.
VOL. 16, No. 2

Are kids facing more life-or-death decisions than ever? Are they being challenged, at earlier ages than before, with scarier choices about drugs, alcohol, sex, and violence? Clearly, most children are growing up in a much more challenging world than we ever imagined. And the consequences of mistakes are more serious than ever!

Of great concern is the fact that many children are not being equipped with the survival skills necessary for making wise decisions about these pressures. More and more seem to believe that bad things can't really happen until after their second or third poor decision. What do I mean? Perhaps an example will best illustrate this point.

Not long ago, I took my son to the movies. As we sat through the multitude of previews and ads for giant-sized, butter-flavored popcorn, I noticed two boys sitting near the front, throwing ice. Their parents were seated about three rows behind them. Mom walked up to them and said something like, "You stop that. I mean it. That's one."

A minute or two later, the ice once again began to sail. This time Dad approached them and said very loudly, "Mom told you to stop that. Now that's two."

Soon, the popcorn began to fly. Dad rushed back down to them and said, "Stop that. If you keep doing that we're going to have to leave!"

Finally, after three or four warnings, these parents put some action behind their threats and took the kids home. What happens when we give children two or three warnings before we deliver a consequence? We condition them to believe that they always can make at least two poor decisions before anything unfortunate happens.

Does this give kids a strong defense against peer pressure? Absolutely not! Why? Because down deep they start to develop "tapes" inside their heads that say things like, "I can smoke crack (or have sex, drink and drive, carry a gun, etc.) at least two times before anything bad happens."

I had a friend in high school with this view. His parents always warned him at least three times before they actually followed through. He lived for a short while believing that nothing bad could happen unless he'd been warned at least twice. Then he died—the first time he went to a party, got drunk, and tried to drive home in a mountain snowstorm. Love and Logic parents know that kids need to understand that bad things can happen after the first poor decision—without repeated warnings.

How do they teach this? They set limits once and follow through with meaningful consequences rather than more warnings.

What's this look like in the movie theater? Mom or Dad walks over and whispers, "Are you guys going to be able to behave or do we need to go?" If the boys act up again, Mom and Dad don't lecture or warn.

Instead, they say something like, "How sad. We're going home now. And by the way, how are you guys going to pay us for the money we spent on tickets, soda, and popcorn? You can tell us later. Try not to worry about it."

© 2000 Charles Fay, Ph.D.

Using Love and Logic Through the Years
By Jim Fay
VOL. 16, NO. 2

"Jim, would it be reasonable that you could get the house painted on the outside by June 1st?" This was Shirley, my wife, speaking to me more than thirty years ago. She was in the process of planting a seed in my mind that remains to this day. That key word was "reasonable."

"I know you like to do the painting yourself since our bad experience with the painter before. Are you sure that's a reasonable time to get it done?"

"Yeah, I guess I could get it painted by then."

Of course, she was asking in November. Things that happen in June usually seem like a good idea in November.

"Now, Jim. Do you want me to remind you? June is a long time off."

"No, I don't need any reminders." I was thinking how much I hate reminders. They just make me mad.

"Are you sure you don't want me to remind you? I don't want you to forget."

"I'll get it done. Don't worry about it."

"Okay, I won't remind you. Thanks for being a good sport about it."

What do you think? Did I forget? You bet I did. That was a long winter. We were raising kids, and I had my hands full at work. June 1st came and went, and the house didn't get painted.

On June 15th I came home from work and found that I couldn't get into my own driveway. A paint contractor's truck was parked there. Ladders were braced on the sides of the house. Painters were busy scraping and painting.

Storming into the house I confronted Shirley. "What is this? You know I like to do our painting. I'm not going to have another painter mess up the place like the last one did!"

"Well, Jim. You said it would be reasonable for you to have the job done by the 1st of June. The job didn't get done."

"But I forgot."

"I know. It's hard to remember, especially with how busy you are. I understand."

"But how are we supposed to pay for this?" I was suddenly very concerned. "One of the reasons I like to do it myself is that we don't have money for this kind of thing!"

"Try not to worry about that, Jim."

Of course this statement made me worry all the more, forcing me to say, "But I am worried. How are we supposed to pay for these professionals?"

"Oh, Jim. You worry too much. I just took the money out of our vacation money. We won't have much of a vacation, but the painters will be paid, and you don't have to worry about the condition of the house."

That did it. To this very day, my ears are especially tuned in to hearing, "Would it be reasonable ... ?" The seed that was planted years ago serves us both very well.

© 2000 Jim Fay

CLINE'S CORNER

Help Your Child to Share
By Foster W. Cline, M.D.

VOL. 16, NO. 2

The joy of sharing develops naturally during elementary school if a child grows up in a loving family who shares. Most children model after their parents and, in addition, sharing is probably a natural instinct that develops normally in most human beings.

But the sharing of toys is certainly not natural in toddlers. The desire to share generally happens around first grade and thereafter when children like making their friends happy. Nevertheless, some parents frustrate themselves by trying to teach sharing to children who are too immature to "get it."

The joy of sharing, like the joy of sex and other instinctual behavior, will occur naturally in most people most of the time.

Even animals tend to share food in tough times. Nobody "taught" them to do it, it just comes naturally.

Sometimes parents who have trouble sharing a 10 percent tithe with the church urge their kids to share considerably more: "You've had an hour playing with your Nintendo. Now let Jamie play for a while."

The same parent might be quite ticked off if someone marched into his home and said, "You've been driving your car all week. Now let someone else drive it for a while."

How to Help Your Child Learn to Share
There are some things parents can do to perhaps ensure that the joy of sharing is instilled in their children, and perhaps even speed up the onset of what probably will develop naturally:

- A home that is loving and respectful of others sets the climate for sharing. Sharing basically says, "I feel happy giving of myself to you." Sharing, then, is an example of a win/win proposition: "Your happiness is my happiness." It's a little difficult to get this picture when a child grows up in an angry, abusive, or win/lose environment.
- Set the model by sharing with your child. Let your child see your pleasure in sharing. Share bites of food off your plate: "Isn't that good! (Smile, smile.) Want another bite?"

  Share of your time: "You know, I think I'd feel great about spending some time with you!"
  Share what you do: "Would you like to carry the package for a while?" or "Would you like to stir for a while?"

- Encourage your child to share. Because the joy of sharing comes from inside, parents defeat the purpose by imposing external demands: "You share with Jenny now!" Sharing develops in the same stages as conscience:

  1. I do it to make my parents happy.

2. I do it to make me happy (because my parents are inside me).

Therefore, the developmental steps or stages as the child grows are:

1. Self-referenced statement: "Boy, I feel good when you share your toy like that!"
2. Kid-referenced statement: "I bet you're happy when you share your candy with Paul."
3. Encourage thinking:
   "Hey, you gave Paul a stick of gum! Why'd you do that?"
   "Because he didn't have any."
   "Really! So you're the type of person who likes to help others out?"
   "Yeah, I guess!"
   "Well, you're a pretty good guesser!"

Although there are things we can do to encourage sharing, one of the best things to do is love your child to pieces. Share with him or her, and watch the joy of sharing develop.

© 2000 Foster W. Cline, M.D.

A Foster Cline Q & A Session

Vol. 16, No. 2

Question

Is the verdict in on playing music for baby in utero?

— Mom-to-Be

Answer

Yes, the verdict is in. Children in utero hear sounds. And they respond to them.

Boris Brott, conductor of the Hamilton, Ontario, Philharmonic Symphony, was interviewed on the radio. After being asked about his interest in music he hesitated for a moment and said:

You know, this may sound strange, but music has been a part of me since before birth. As a young man I was mystified by this unusual ability I had—to play certain pieces sight unseen. I would be conducting a score for the first time and, suddenly, the cello line would jump out at me; I'd know the flow of the piece before I would turn the page of the score.

One day, I mentioned this to my mother, who is a professional cellist. I thought she would be intrigued because it was always the cello line that was so distinct in my mind. She was, but when she heard what the pieces were, the mystery quickly solved itself. All the scores I knew, sight unseen, were ones she had played while she was pregnant with me. (Reported by Verny)

In Evergreen, Colorado, Melody, a young mother, remembers the gestation and infancy of her firstborn child:

During Troy's pregnancy, I was musical chairman at the church. There was one piece that was difficult and I practiced singing it and playing it on the guitar, over and over again. I practiced to the point of being sick of it, and after the church service, I never played it again.

Months later, Troy was born, and months after that, one night, he was fussy and I picked up the guitar and started singing. He remained fussy. Then I started singing, with no forethought at all, the song I had practiced during my pregnancy.

It was magic! He immediately calmed down. Once, before his second birthday, out of the blue, he came up and put his head on my lap and said, "Mommy, that's my favorite song!"

© 2000 Foster W. Cline, M.D.

Poor Decisions More Costly for Today's Teens—Survey
Love and Logic Institute
VOL. 16, NO. 2

Three out of four American adults believe today's youth face more dangerous decisions than they did as teens, according to a new survey of 1,015 American adults released by the Love and Logic Press, Inc.

Adults responding to the survey saw a variety of negative influences on children, choosing television (29 percent), peers (27 percent), and the Internet (19 percent) as the leading culprits.

Only 11 percent believe teenagers' decision-making ability has improved from a generation ago. Forty-four percent believe it has worsened.

More than half of the respondents believe children are first tempted to experiment with drugs, alcohol, and sex before the age of fourteen.

And while 41 percent think peers influence children and teens about the same amount today as a generation ago, a full 46 percent believe friends have a greater influence on today's youth.

The Love and Logic Press commissioned the survey as part of its ongoing efforts to understand the state of child care in America and to help adults become more successful teachers and parents.

"This environment has the potential to create a stressful and chaotic life for kids and their parents, but the Love and Logic philosophy cuts through the negative clutter and makes parenting and teaching fun and rewarding," says Jim Fay, cofounder of the Love and Logic Press and coauthor of the national bestseller *Parenting with Love and Logic.*

The survey also included a series of parenting questions that ranged from what to do when feeding a fussy toddler to how to handle a teenager's speeding ticket.

The answers were tied to four very different parenting styles defined by the Love and Logic Press: the Drill Sergeant, the Hovering Helicopter, the Anything Goes Parent, and the Consultant (Love and Logic) Parent.

Given these four types of choices, most adults (57 percent) responded to the parenting questions inconsistently, although they were most likely to select approaches that protect a child from negative consequences.

While respondents struggled with how to consistently raise and discipline children, they did agree (92 percent strongly or somewhat agreed) that young children who make small decisions are better prepared to make big decisions when they are older.

"That's the key," Fay says. "Today parenting is all over the place, and that can exhaust an adult's patience. Love and Logic helps put the fun back into parenting.

"Children who grow in responsibility also will grow in self-esteem, and I can't think of two better reasons to celebrate."

For more information about the survey, please visit the Love and Logic website at www.loveandlogic.com or call 800-LUV-LOGIC.

© 2000 Love and Logic Institute

A Spoiled Brat in Training
By Jim Fay
Vol. 16, No. 3

"Take it off! Take it off now! I want it off!"

"Not now, okay?"

"Take it off!"

"Please wait till we get on the plane, okay?" Dad continued his pleading, to no avail.

"Take it off! Take it off! Take it off! I want it off now!" demanded three-year-old Lydia.

Lydia was talking about an identification tag on her little roller-bag luggage. It was obvious to those in the boarding area that she was used to getting her way. It was also obvious that her loving parents were dedicated to serving her every demand.

Her parents appeared to be very kind people who talked to her with great respect, much as servants would respond to the Queen. They never raised their voices. They used all their words of respect—"please," "thank you," etc. Her every request was their command. Sadly, they set no limits on her behavior.

I'm sure if I had asked them about their child-rearing practices, they would have told me they were dedicated to making sure Lydia was never frustrated, thus ensuring that she would grow up secure and confident.

Little do these parents know that treating Lydia as an honored guest in the home will have the opposite effect of developing a wonderful person with high self-concept.

Treating kids like royalty produces people who learn to get their way through anger and demands. They come to believe that temper tantrums and demands are the only way to get what they want.

It saddens me to know that the day will come when we will hear Lydia's parents complaining, "I can't understand this. We've never asked anything of her. We gave her everything she wanted and now look how she treats us. Why can't she ever appreciate what we do for her?"

Little three-year-old Lydia barks orders and her parents, like robots, jump to do her bidding. As she screamed, "Take it off!" I watched her father reach down and do exactly what she ordered. As he removed the identification tag he said, "Can you ask in a nice voice, okay?"

You can guess that Lydia didn't do as he asked. Why should she? She got her way using her nasty voice. Why change something that works so well?

Instead of asking in a nice voice, she launched right into her next command, which was, "Put it in my suitcase. I want it in my suitcase."

"I'll keep it for you. You don't need it in the suitcase, okay?"

"No! I want it in my suitcase! I want it in there now!"

Without a word, Dad opened the suitcase and did as he was ordered. And at this time I desperately wanted to say, "Dad, you've been well trained by that three-year-old. You have fallen into a deadly pattern that will create a self-centered, insecure child who only feels important when she's getting her way. I can also predict that it will become increasingly difficult for you to satisfy her demands as she grows into her teen years. How sad for both parents and child."

If Dad were to ask for my help, I'd also call his attention to his use of the word "okay." Notice that each time he makes a statement to Lydia he ends the sentence with the word "okay," followed with a question mark. It gives Lydia the impression that he is constantly asking for her approval.

The Retraining Process

Fortunately it's not too late for the parents to retrain little Lydia. A step-by-step process can turn Lydia into a nice little person who knows her limits and has some manners.

Step One: Start the training process in the home, where parents have the most control. Pay close attention to Lydia's demands. The parents should ignore them:

LYDIA: "I want candy."
PARENT: (Totally ignores Lydia.)
LYDIA: "I want it right now!"
PARENT: (Totally ignores Lydia.)
LYDIA: "I need my candy right now!"
PARENT: "Lydia, have you figured out why we're not listening to you? Thank you."
LYDIA: "But it's time for my candy!"

Step Two: Parent immediately uses the, "Uh, Oh Song" technique. "Uh, oh. A little bedroom time coming up. How sad."

Lydia is immediately whisked off to her room and stays there until she is sweet, regardless of the fit she throws in her room. As soon as she is calm, *and never before,* the parents set the egg timer for four minutes and Lydia's job is to remain calm for four consecutive minutes.

She is then allowed to come out. The parents remember not to lecture about her behavior. Lydia will soon figure out what is causing her trips to the room, provided her parents consistently use this technique each time she acts out.

The "Uh, Oh Song" technique can be learned on the *Toddlers and Preschoolers* audiotape, available through the Love and Logic Institute. This training technique is also offered in the book *Love and Logic Magic for Early Childhood.*

Step Three: The training sessions are taken away from the house. These sessions are well planned in advance and require the help of a good neighbor or friend who is known by Lydia.

The parents take Lydia to the store. The neighbor or friend follows the family and is available to help at a moment's notice, but remains out of sight. All the adults are secretly hoping that Lydia will decide to test the limits in a new place.

When Lydia starts to act up, one parent asks, "Lydia, do you think it's wise for you to be acting like that?"

If Lydia doesn't shape up immediately, the parent sings the "Uh, Oh Song." "Uh, oh. A little bedroom time is coming up. How sad."

The youngster is carried to the waiting helper as the parent says, "Lydia needs to go to her room. She can come out when we get home. I'm sure she has some toys that she can use to pay you for your help. Thank you."

Notice the finer points of this session:

- The parents can control when and where the training takes place.
- The helper is not a stranger to the youngster.
- The parents can return home in a timely fashion, thus controlling the amount of time Lydia is in her room.
- The parents display no anger or frustration over the behavior.
- Lydia quickly learns that demands and manipulation get different results than she is looking for.

- The parents can be prepared for a follow-up session if necessary. Parents should continue to use the "Uh, Oh Song" whenever necessary.

A common concern raises the question, "How is Lydia going to learn to do the right thing?" It is hoped the parents are demonstrating the correct way to make requests as they treat each other with the words of respect. It is also helpful to know that little children are experimenters by nature. They keep experimenting with new ways when what they have used doesn't work.

The good news is that this child, who was well on her way to becoming a tyrant, can become a blessing.

© 2000 Jim Fay

Love and Logic Treats Both Symptoms and Causes
By Charles Fay, Ph.D.

VOL. 16, NO. 3

Fourteen-year-old Curtis walks in from school, throws his coat on the floor, and immediately begins the fine art of verbal brain drain: "Mom! I'm starvin'. What's for dinner?"

Mother greets him with a smile and says, "Honey, we're having leftovers from last night—meatloaf. How was school?"

Faster than the speed of light, Curtis's eyes roll back in his head, his jaw drops, and he whines, "Aw, Mom! I don't waaaant thaaaaat. Let's get pizza. I hate meatloaf!"

Full battle shields deployed, and her once sweet smile fading, Mom enters the fray. "No! We are not going out tonight. What do you think? Do you think money grows on trees?"

By the time they both sit down for dinner, Mom is exhausted, Curtis has experienced an entertaining show of parental frustration and anger, and another chunk of their relationship has been damaged.

What's the good news here? For more than twenty years, Love and Logic has helped thousands of parents bring the fun back into raising kids.

Why have the techniques had such lasting and widespread success? Largely because Love and Logic treats both symptoms (misbehavior) and underlying causes (children's need for love, healthy control, to be noticed, and self-esteem).

Symptoms? Causes? What does all of this really mean? Let's imagine that the mother above has two trusted friends who fashion themselves as rather accomplished amateur child therapists.

She consults with friend number one, who responds, "Make his arguing backfire for him. Until he stops this habit, try going on strike. Each time he asks you for something, say, 'I'll be happy to do these things for you when I feel treated with respect.'"

Not bad for an amateur! On her way home, she stops by the store and runs into friend number two. Mom throws the question his way. What's his answer? "You need to find out why he's arguing so much in the first place. Does he feel connected to you in a loving way? Is he crying out for attention, some control, or some loving limits? Is he feeling really poorly about himself?"

Not bad for an amateur! There's only one problem. Now Mom is really confused. What does she do? Does she just deliver a consequence? Or does she find and treat the causes of Curtis's arguing escapades? Which friend is correct?

Both and neither! Using a good, logical consequence, alone, often stops the misbehavior. What's the problem then? If the child's underlying needs are not met, the misbehavior tends to resurface later—either in its original form or in some other. Arguing may return as arguing—or as a quiet refusal to do what the parent asks.

Treating causes, alone, also falls short of the mark. While the child may start to feel much better because his or her emotional needs are being met, the misbehavior continues because it's become such a habit.

Powerful and lasting solutions
address both symptoms and
underlying needs.

What would happen if we had a machine that could combine two human beings? What would happen if we combined the two amateur therapist friends above? Who would we have?

Simply stated, we'd have a master of Love and Logic! Now, let's imagine that Mom took this person's advice. Mom's plan would likely have two parts.

Mom's Plan Part One: Treat the Symptom

She'd begin by whispering in a sad tone of voice, "This is so sad. I'll be happy to listen when your voice sounds like mine. And, by the way, I do things for people who treat me with respect."

Most kids learn quickly that arguing gets them nothing while being respectful gets them a lot.

Mom's Plan Part Two: Treat the Underlying Causes

Love and Logic parents simply meet universal human needs. These needs, the underlying causes of most behaviors, include:

• The need for unconditional love, respect, and comforting limits.

Love and Logic parents meet this need by wrapping consequences in a strong blanket of empathy: "This is so sad. I know you must be really mad. And I'll be happy to take you out for pizza when I know we won't have an argument."

The underlying message is, "I will always value and love you, even when I don't like your behavior."

• The need for healthy control.

When children are angry, defiant, or resentful, they are actually hurting. Giving them plenty of healthy choices is medicine for their wounds.

The mother above would give Curtis lots of choices like, "Do you want to have juice or milk for dinner?" "Are you going to set your alarm for 6:00 or 6:15?" "Would you like to have your hair long or short?"

• The need to be noticed and to feel good about oneself.

During tough times, kids need more than ever for us to see their strengths and point these out. Sadly, we often forget to do this when we are caught up in the problem.

Our Love and Logic mom would greet her son each morning and evening with a high-five, a hug, and a smile. She also takes time out to notice positives.

If we were a fly on the wall, we'd see and hear her saying things like, "Curtis, I noticed your friends really look up to you." "Curtis, I noticed you really take pride in your skateboarding." "Curtis, I noticed you like to draw."

It's amazing what we will do to please the people who notice our strengths!

• • •

A middle-school teacher gave a wonderful example of how powerful this two-part approach can be. She had tried every logical consequence in the book to keep one of her students from skipping class.

Nothing seemed to work with this extremely challenging boy until she also began focusing on underlying needs. One afternoon, when she was sure that he had run away from the school, she got the surprise of her life!

Walking into her class and smiling, he said, "Hey! I bet you thought I left. You can't get rid of me that easy." All that made the difference were some simple smiles, an occasional handshake, some small choices, and a focus on the good side rather than the bad!

© 2000 Charles Fay, Ph.D.

CLINE'S CORNER

The Art of Micro Love and Logic
By Foster W. Cline, M.D.
VOL. 16, NO. 3

A few years ago, a friend and his wife, who had a basically neat but sometimes ill-mannered little four-year-old tike, visited my wife and me.

They said, "We know Jake is a handful too much of the time. And we know he has ADD. And we know he is strong-willed. But we also know that our parenting techniques could use improvement. Would you and Hermie, when you see Jake being difficult, just handle it, so we can watch you."

What wonderful people. What a gift! To be given a free hand to demonstrate to friends how to handle a difficult child! So often we all are in the position of "wishing we could say something," but (1) it's not that big a deal; (2) the parents didn't ask for our input; (3) even if we gave it, they might be resentful or not use it. Love and Logic teaches that almost all unasked-for advice is taken as criticism.

After a week with us, Jake truly was a different child. Our friends told us that they watched us use "micromanagement." What in the world did they mean by that? They said it wasn't in the way my wife and I handled the big blowups, it was in the everyday small interchanges that they saw techniques that made a difference.

So together we sat down and looked at the principles that they discovered—principles we didn't even know we were using. I'm passing on these micro Love and Logic responses in the hopes they may be helpful to other parents.

1. When relating to little kids, have a mobile face, smile, and comment on the things they do well with pizzazz. All discipline is based on having a good relationship with the child. Your approval or disapproval has to *matter!*

2. When the children are being obnoxious, truly ignore 'em. Don't look at them, don't respond, don't say, "I don't like that," "I'll be with you in a minute," or "Just a sec." Turn off. Truly turn off.

3. When the child continues and escalates to the point of being hard to ignore, firmly request that the child go sit on a chair until you tell him or her to get up. Be *very* firm but not angry. Mean business without being mean.

4. Choices are everywhere:

"Would you like to finish your dinner now, or wait until breakfast to eat?"

"Would you like to cry in your room with your door open or scream with your door closed?"

"Would you like to talk more softly to me, or talk more loudly to the mirror in your room?"

"Would you like to quiet down and go in the car with us, or would you prefer to be noisy with a baby-sitter?" (**Only** said if you mean the choice and are willing to say it only once and call the sitter *immediately*.)

"Would you like to give your choice of where you would like to go to eat without whining, or would you like me to pick the restaurant?"

Thus the child quickly learns that he or she gets emotions for doing things right, no emotion whatsoever for goofing up, and firm isolation for doing things wrong or being obnoxious.

Most choices are easy and not nearly so controlling: "Would you like to eat your peaches or your beets first?" Almost any order a parent feels like giving a child can be stated with a sentence that begins with "Would," which gives the child a choice.

5. If the child is young and a little hyperactive, turn off the TV and give the child tasks to focus on. Sit and do the tasks with the child, making it fun with your presence. Then expect the child to do the tasks him- or herself:

• Cover a chair with masking tape that will pull right off.
• Sew buttons.
• String beads.

- Do a hooked rug.
- Build with Legos.
- Cut pictures from magazines.
- String together paper-towel and toilet-paper cardboard tubes and paint them.

When children are toddlers, they must learn that parents have the power, and that they only use it when verbal requests are ignored. A child's feeling of personal power can only come from parents modeling the correct use of personal power before the child is old enough for it to be a power struggle.

Angry children who hurt others almost never have parents who model the correct use of quiet, non-frustrated-sounding personal power. Personal power correctly modeled is not:

- Noisy
- Demanding
- Frustrated
- Pleading
- Whining

It is:

- Firmness with the expectation of compliance
- Authoritative
- Loving
- Enabling
- Used without warning

Good luck. If these techniques worked with Jake, they'll work with your child!

© 2000 Foster W. Cline, M.D.

A Foster Cline Q & A Session

Vol. 16, No. 3

Question

My two-year-old is heading back to preschool soon and I'm worried because he has developed a habit of biting people. What should we do?

— Worried Mom

Answer

Biting in toddlerhood is a "stage." If the child is small, it is usually sufficient just to say no *firmly* and remove the child from the scene for a bit. Usually ten to fifteen minutes will do it. One minute per year of age is simply not long enough.

The main thing is to handle the situation quickly, efficiently, and without showing undue frustration. (Children love a frustrated adult!) If the child obeys most commands and is generally responsive and loving, he or she will almost certainly outgrow the problem within a few months at most. If the child is basically noncompliant, won't stay isolated, and has other behavioral difficulties, then acquiring professional help may be indicated.

© 2000 Foster W. Cline, M.D.

What Do You Value?

By Jim Fay

Vol. 16, No. 4

Are you more interested in your child's grade-point average or his/her character and personal responsibility? Pat yourself on the back if you answered "character and responsibility."

Children who grow up in homes where character and responsibility are modeled, valued, and enforced most often have little trouble being successful in school and in their future lives.

I recently had a call from a parent who was concerned about her teenager's lying. After some discussion, Mom admitted the teen had stolen a credit card and purchased items over the Internet. However, Mom's major concern was about the lying, not the criminal behavior.

Several times this mother said, "I just don't want him to have a record." In desperation, I finally asked, "Are you saying you don't mind that he's a criminal as long as he doesn't look like a criminal?"

"Well, no. But this is going to be so hard for him. What do I do?"

Would I be wrong to guess that you, the reader, have no problem figuring out what this mother needs to do? Isn't it always easier to know what other parents should do about their misbehaving children?

She needs to treat this teenage mistake as an opportunity for her son to develop character through facing his responsibilities and their consequences. The problem for most of us is not knowing what is right, it's having the backbone to do it in the face of watching our children experience the pain of mistakes and consequences.

Further discussion with this distraught parent revealed a typical history. Her son often made mistakes while Mom found ways to prevent or deflect the natural outcomes. Mother was quick to blame the influences of her child's friends. She was quick to blame the school when bad report cards came home. This unfortunate youngster was systematically trained that Mom would stand between his misbehavior and real-world consequences.

Another parent was concerned about her eleventh-grade daughter who was an honor student, but who had admitted being truant six times during the school quarter. Mom was concerned because the school's policy stated that six unexcused absences resulted in automatic failing grades and a requirement to repeat the classes.

Her daughter told her not to worry, that she had taken care of the problem. It turned out she had forged Mom's signature excusing the absences. She then quickly added, "Now, Mom. You can't tell the teachers."

"Why?" Mom asked.

"Mom, if you tell, I'll fail the quarter. Then I won't be an honor student anymore. And you want me to be an honor student, don't you?"

Isn't it amazing that, as a reader, you have no problem knowing what this mother should do? This situation with her teen is a character issue. She needs to take advantage of the opportunity to hold her daughter accountable for her actions. No child should grow up with the belief that parents will stand between misbehavior and the world's natural consequences.

The picture that's so clear to you and me was not so clear for this parent. Her picture of the situation was clouded with doubt and conflict. She didn't want her daughter to suffer, nor did she want to discourage her teen from telling the truth. But what this mother needed most of all was a way to hold her child accountable while still maintaining her trust and love.

Don't Fall Into Traps
This is an easy trap for parents to fall into. We love our children. When we think of them being uncomfortable or hurting, we hurt even more than they do.

It helps to remember that our attempts to protect children from the consequences of their mistakes often have more to do with comforting and protecting ourselves. Holding children accountable for their actions requires a higher level of love than the love required to protect them from discomfort or accountability.

Both of these mothers had fallen into another trap. They had bought into a belief that childhood self-concept is damaged when kids make mistakes and experience the consequences. Nothing could be further from the truth. Self-concept is damaged every time parents excuse bad behavior.

Do the Right Thing and Be Loved for It
Love and Logic gives us a great solution for this dilemma. There is a way of holding kids responsible for their actions without appearing mean. This wonderful technique leaves kids thinking, "My parent is not my problem. My bad decisions are my problem."

Give your children a heavy dose of empathy or compassion before laying down any kind of punishment or consequence. This opens their minds and hearts to learn from their mistakes without blaming you.

Let's see how the first teenager's mother might help her son face the natural consequences of making purchases with a stolen credit card. She needs to resist her temptation to react in anger, which will only make her youngster defensive.

A Heavy Dose of Empathy

Let's give the mother some skills for helping her son do the right thing. You and I know it will probably be harder on her than it is on the teenager. We also know he will initially be very angry with her.

However, this is the day that he will start walking a long path toward respecting and loving her. The day eventually will come when he will say, "Mom, remember when you made me face the music about the credit card? That was the day you made a man out of me. Thanks."

Here are the words she can use:

MOM: "Oh, Sweetie. What a bummer. My heart goes out to you. What a problem. I bet you just feel awful. Would it help if I went to the police with you and held your hand while you explain this?"

TEEN: "But, Mom. It's not fair! Can't you just get me a lawyer?"

MOM: (holds the line in a loving way) "Sweetie, I love you too much to let you pass up this opportunity to learn about how the real world works." (Mom needs to repeat this statement for each new argument the child tries, and there will be many.)

TEEN: "But, Mom!"

MOM: "Sweetie, I told you I love you too much to argue. Thank you."

Mom now needs to remove herself and allow the teen to deal with his own anger. Continuing to discuss it at this time will only lead to more problems.

This is a sad story about a mother and son who are both paying a huge price. Neither of these people would be in this situation had Mom started early, handling the little problems and misbehaviors in this manner. It's the Love and Logic way.

A Little Boredom Is a Good Thing
By Charles Fay, Ph.D.
Vol. 16, No. 4

This is boooring. I don't got nothin' to dooo!

How often does the average parent hear these words? Have times ever changed! I mean, when I was a kid my parents trained me real quick never to utter the words "bored" or "boring." Any complaints made about not having enough to do were always greeted with an exuberant, "Oh goodie, here's a mop" or "Super! I've been wondering who was going to stack that wood outside. Thanks!"

I was lucky. Now I realize that. Not only did they help me feel good about myself, by teaching me how to work hard, they also modeled wonderful things.

I never heard them complain about boredom. Instead, I watched them be creative with their spare time. My father played his trombone, helped me with my tree house, or refinished old furniture. My mom did crosswords, read books, and sewed.

As a family we cleaned, fixed our old broken cars, remodeled the house, fished, pulled weeds, stacked wood, and talked a lot. Even the chores I look back on with fondness, simply because it felt good to be useful and it was fun to be with my parents.

Is happiness an inside or outside job? A major shift in thinking has taken place in America. There was a time not that long ago when most people saw it as their personal responsibility to keep *themselves* entertained. They didn't spend much time complaining about being bored or not having enough to do. Instead, they viewed happiness as an inside job—something only one's self could achieve through hard work and struggle.

Now it seems that many people view happiness as an outside job. Sadly, they constantly look for external sources of excitement to fill their lives. Being alone is viewed as a curse. Quiet moments are to be avoided at all costs. Boredom is the worst. Many seem to reason, "Why be creative when it takes so much work?"

A little boredom is a very good thing. It is through the process of finding oneself in a dull situation, being forced to think creatively, and finding a way of entertaining oneself that children develop many of the skills necessary for academic, occupational, and interpersonal success.

Creative problem-solving, patience, and the value of delayed gratification are all assets honed by "boring moments." Where would we be today if people like Ben Franklin, Thomas Edison, and Marie Curie had never found themselves in dull situations?

In a society that regards boredom as horrible, is it possible that many children will memorize the lines of television sitcoms yet never reach their creative, academic, or emotional potentials?

What do kids need—healthy stimulation or entertainment? What has contributed to this change of thinking? Why does it seem that so many people believe that it is someone *else's* responsibility to make them happy and keep them entertained?

One major cause has to do with confusion between healthy stimulation and entertainment. Research clearly shows that healthy stimulation is essential for proper development. Children who don't receive enough loving touch, aren't talked to enough, never have their parents read them stories, and don't have opportunities to engage in creative play, are at great risk for physical, emotional, and academic problems.

The hallmark of healthy stimulation is that it involves some type of positive interaction between the child and environment—an interaction that creates learning and growth. Children learn and grow from stacking blocks and knocking them down. Children learn and grow from hearing Grandpa talk about the good old days. Children learn and grow from sawing wood and nailing it together. They learn and grow from drawing silly pictures, and seeing their parents giggle. They learn and grow from creating dramas between rag dolls and army men.

Unfortunately, many parents, and some professionals, have become confused about the difference between this type of stimulation and entertainment. Stimulation requires active thought, participation, or human interaction. Entertainment, in contrast, simply involves watching or interacting with an object in a passive manner.

As a result of this confusion, many parents have come to believe two things. First, it is horrible if their children become bored. And second, it is their job as good parents to make sure that their children are constantly entertained. In their homes, children have all the latest video games and videos, need a never-ending supply of batteries to power their other toys, ride from one activity to the next in minivans with built-in television sets, and never learn how to struggle, make creative discoveries, or delay gratification. As a result, they lack what it takes to be successful and happy at school. Some eventually become labeled as learning-disabled, ADHD, or simply "a pain."

The great news is that this *does not have to happen!* There are some very practical and fun ways of helping kids learn to face boredom with creativity rather than complaints. An added bonus is that parents learn that they don't have to run circles around their kids trying to keep them happy.

Give yourself and your kids a break. Here's how.

Teach Your Kids That Happiness Comes from Doing Things Rather Than Getting Things

This happens most effectively when children are expected to do chores, and they see their parents doing them, as well. Modeling is the key.

Some parents shoot themselves in the foot by complaining about their chores in front of the kids—or being grumpy when their kids are helping them. But doing chores together as a family, talking about the satisfaction it brings you, and being silly in the process, are all ways of helping children learn to take pride in working.

I know a family where the parents have made it a ritual for each member to be involved in making dinner, serving it, and cleaning up. Singing, giggling, and participating are about the only rules. Sometimes the food quality reflects this joy. Other times it doesn't. What's important are the interactions and the love.

A second way of teaching this healthy value is by requiring children to earn what they want. Marc, my seven-year-old son, recently asked me for a bike lock. I could have bought it for him. It was only five dollars. Instead, I asked him, "How are you going to earn it?"

With some guidance, he replied, "Maybe do extra chores?" After he spent plenty of time and effort cleaning the garage, I placed the lock in his hands and said, "Thanks so much! You really earned this." He spent the rest of the week smiling, working the combination over and over, and repeating, "I earned it myself. I earned it myself."

Isn't it ironic that kids often grumble about doing chores—the very activities that help them feel the best about themselves?

Have Some "Boredom Training Sessions"

Since learning how to deal creatively with dull situations is so key to lifelong success, doesn't it make sense that we create some rather monotonous moments, allow our kids to get "bored," and then guide them toward owning and solving this problem for themselves?

In our modern era, with all of its wonderful electronic distractions, it's become essential that parents actually engineer situations that require their kids to delay gratification, use self-control, think creatively, and find their own entertainment.

Steps for Creating a Boredom Training Session

Step 1: Provide at least thirty minutes of dullness each day.

Step 2: Provide this time when you are best prepared to deal with a bored child.

Step 3: If your child says, "I'm bored," hand the problem back in a loving way.

Here's an example of how a parent might apply these steps:

CHILD: "I'm bored. Can I watch TV?"

PARENT: "Sure. You can watch TV in half an hour. I think it would be nice to have some quiet time until then."

CHILD: "But why? I don't have anything to do."

PARENT: (delivers a strong dose of empathy and hands the problem back) "Oh. That's got to be hard. What are you going to do?"

CHILD: "How about video games? Or maybe we could go to the movies?"

PARENT: "You can play video games in thirty minutes. Would you like to hear some other ideas?"

CHILD: "What?"

PARENT: "Some kids decide to do chores for a while. How would that work?"

CHILD: "Awful."

PARENT: "Some kids decide to draw pictures, play in the sand outside, or make something out of wood. How would that work?"

CHILD: "Boring."

PARENT: "Some kids decide to play catch or some other game with their mom or dad. How would that work?"

CHILD: (rolling his eyes) "Well, okay. Can we make that rocket thing out of vinegar and baking soda again?"

PARENT: "Sure! This time, let's point it away from Dad."

More and more people are falling into the trap of believing that happiness comes from getting good things. At the Love and Logic Institute, we believe that happiness comes from doing good things.

The great news is that parents can take some simple yet very powerful steps to help their children learn this lesson early in their lives. Each time this lesson is repeated, our children receive something that nobody can ever take from them—inner joy!

For many other helpful parenting and teaching remedies, see *Love and Logic Magic: When Kids Leave You Speechless,* by Jim Fay and Charles Fay, Ph.D.

CLINE'S CORNER

Building Character and Discipline in Children
By Foster W. Cline, M.D.

VOL. 16, NO. 4

All parents want to raise children who show self-discipline and character. But many parents go about it in the wrong way. They think they can somehow demand or force their children to show character. That is like gluing wings on a caterpillar to produce a butterfly!

Actually, producing a butterfly calls for more natural responses than gluing on wings! In the right environment with God and time, it just happens. That is the way it is in developing character in children.

If children are given the right parental input, they naturally develop character. Nobody has to talk about it. Nobody has to insist on it. It just happens!

Those who live a fulfilling life don't start out with the goal, "I want to live a fulfilling life." Parents of children with character may seldom consciously attempt to build character.

A fulfilling life naturally happens as individual little choices are made day after day. Character builds in the hundred little daily steps as parents interact with their child. Children cannot be lectured or cajoled into developing character.

So how is character built? Character is something that shows from *inside the skin*. But all the elements of character are first *demonstrated* outside the skin through parental *expectations*. In essence, what children experience outside their skin becomes what they show from the inside.

The foundation for character development generally happens in the first years of life. When character is built in the later years, an adult, teen, or even school-age child must go through some very tough life experiences to develop it. These are traumatic experiences through which they survive, stretch, and grow.

Character is built in the early years in precise age-specific steps.

Year One: Foundation for Character

A person of character has the ability to do what is right. He or she has an internal guidance system. But to have these qualities three elements must be present:

- Basic trust
- Causal thinking—giving the ability to plan ahead
- Foundation for conscience

The foundation for all three elements is laid down in the first year of life.

Basic trust develops when parents, during the first year of life, teach children, "You can count on me." (Later, as the beliefs of the parents are internalized, and the child comes to see himself as the parents see him, he says, "I can count on myself, and others can count on me.")

Causal thinking develops when parents are consistent. The child learns, "Mom is hustling in the kitchen, I'll eat soon." Or, "Dad is putting on my coat, so we must be going somewhere."

The *foundation for conscience* is laid when the child learns during the first year, "When Mom is upset, I'm upset." Or, "Smiling parents mean good things for me."

External discipline, which will become, after the process of internalizing the parents, *self-discipline,* starts in the first year. Character always involves self-discipline. Correct parental discipline becomes self-discipline. The way the parents treat the infant and toddler becomes the way they treat themselves. The foundation for discipline is built by how the parents handle "Don't touch" or "No" and temper tantrums.

"Don't touch" and "No" have to do with learning, "Do you do what others expect?" Temper tantrums have to do with learning, "Do you act nice around others?"

Amazing as it may sound, by the end of the first year, the child has built an important foundation for character formation:

He or she has *basic trust* and thinks others are important.

He or she has *causal thinking* and the foundation for logical conclusions and planning ahead.

He or she has the *foundation for conscience* and knows that how others feel affects him.

Year Two: Foundation for Self-Discipline

During the second year of life, children learn that:

• Parents have certain loving expectations.

• They must meet those expectations.

If expectations of adults are not met, negative consequences will follow—consequences that they must learn to accept.

It is during the second year that children of character learn it is not okay to be obnoxious and demanding. Correct parenting requires that children show the parents respect, and this becomes internalized as *self-respect*. Correct parental discipline during the second year is the nucleus around which the pearl of *self-discipline* develops.

Thus during the second year, children who are allowed to be disrespectful to parents become disrespectful of themselves and develop a poor self-image. Individuals of character inevitably have high self-images because they have met their own reasonable expectations, which were *first learned as reasonable parental expectations*.

Summing up, the second year revolves around respect and obeying the loving authority of parents. This becomes high self-image, self-respect, and self-control.

Now we are ready for the last element of character.

Years Three and Four: Pride in Accomplishment

Individuals of character tend to be self-motivated achievers who have pride in their accomplishments. Children learn the excitement of accomplishing things in the last half of the second year through the third and fourth years of life.

Accomplishment is a "doing" word. Accomplishment implies *action*. Accomplishment is the opposite of passivity. *Watching TV brings about passivity, not action.* Motivation, pride in accomplishment, and excitement when achieving are endangered when children spend more time watching something than doing something during the first four and a half years of life.

During this time period, many parents mistakenly believe that watching "quality programs for children" is not detrimental or might even be helpful to their children. This is not true. The children, watching TV, do not learn:

- Self-motivation
- Pride in achievement
- Task focus
- Concentration on internally determined constructs
- Gross motor developmental skills
- Expressive communication skills
- Socially appropriate behavior

TV may *show* all of the above, but the child does not *experience* these elements. Experience is the great teacher! As one mom noted, "Watching June Cleaver never helped me become a better mom."

In summary, a person of character has basic trust in others, conscience, the ability to plan ahead, self-discipline and self-respect, and pride in accomplishment. Surprisingly, all of these things are learned very early in a child's life—during infancy, toddlerhood, and early childhood!

With this foundation, the children are ready to use the values that the parents teach. If the above foundation is not present, children are not able to learn values, which run off them like water off a duck's back!

Empathy opens the heart and mind for learning.

© *2001 Foster W. Cline, M.D.*

VOLUME
17

If Kids Can Hear Promises, They Can Hear Requests

By Jim Fay

Vol. 17, No. 1

You can train your child to hear you the first time you say something. Or you can train him or her to ignore you. Raising a child who listens to adults is a source of joy. Raising one who doesn't is a constant source of frustration and torment.

Our actions either train kids to listen or train them not to listen. Consider this situation I witnessed in the airport recently. Joshua, a five-year-old, was running out into the concourse.

"Joshua, you stop that running!" called his mother. She did not follow through, so Joshua continued dashing in and out of a crowd of irritated travelers.

"Joshua, you get over here!" Once more, she barked an order, but did nothing to enforce it.

"Joshua! Get off that!" Another order was shouted by Mom and ignored by Joshua.

Suddenly Joshua was right at my feet staring up at me.

Mother ordered again, "Joshua, you get away from that man. You come over here. Quit bothering people."

I looked down at Joshua and asked, "Joshua, what's your mom going to do if you don't do what she says?"

He knew the answer immediately, "Nothing."

Of course, he was right. He had been trained by his mother that she could bark orders, but would never enforce them. Why should he listen if the results of not listening meant he could do as he pleased without adult interference?

Joshua never had to come to his mother. She came over to him, held his hand, and apologized with, "I'm so sorry. You know how five-year-olds are. They won't listen to a thing you say."

I can't tell you how much restraint it took for me to keep from saying, "I've known a lot of five-year-olds who listen to their parents. But their parents mean what they say."

Training kids to listen is not brain surgery. It's not complicated. Joshua's mom could retrain him to listen by first of all retraining herself to do the following:

1. Make a commitment that she will never repeat herself. Kids unconsciously learn how many times each parent will repeat a request before taking action. She can give Joshua the gift of knowing that she will only say something once.
2. Be prepared to act. She needs to be dedicated to making her child's life somewhat uncomfortable each time he fails to listen the first time she says something. This means that as soon as he disobeys, she goes to him and takes him back to his seat and makes him stay with her, saying, "How sad not to listen. Now you can stay with me."
3. She should never accept "But I didn't hear you" as an excuse. When confronted with this excuse, she responds with, "How sad not to be listening. Maybe your ears will get better." It is important that she follows through with the consequences of not listening.
4. Be prepared for Joshua to have a fit about not getting his way. Even though this will be uncomfortable, other adults around her will secretly applaud her courage and willingness to put forth effort to raise a well-behaved child.

I have worked with kids and families for forty-seven years. During this time I have never met a child who failed to hear a parent's promise. They always hear promises the first time.

I've also learned that their ears work the same way for requests when parents learn and follow the four steps. Training and expecting kids to listen is one of a parent's greatest gifts. It's the Love and Logic way.

It's not too late for Joshua's mom to retrain him to listen.

© 2001 Jim Fay

Positive Relationships: Reaching Tough Students
By Charles Fay, Ph.D.

Vol. 17, No. 1

What is the most powerful teaching skill for reaching tough kids? If teachers were allowed only one tool for motivating students with chips on their shoulders, what would most choose?

Traveling across the country, I've had the blessed opportunity to ask thousands of highly experienced and highly skilled teachers to ponder these two questions. I'm always amazed by how fast and how confidently they respond, and I'm always stunned by how similar their answers are. What have I learned from this research?

Master teachers, particularly those teaching very challenging students, say things like, "The most important skill is being firm but getting to know the kids so they know I care," or "Respect. They have to know that I care about them and their lives beyond the classroom."

It's clear that most experienced teachers view the ability to develop positive relationships, trust, and rapport as being the most important, crucial skill for reaching challenging students.

But what do they mean when they say the words "relationship," "trust," or "rapport"? When I ask them to be more specific, they describe a balance between being strict with high expectations and being very friendly and caring.

In a nutshell, this is what the Love and Logic approach is all about—giving adults skills that allow them to be strict and loving at the same time.

Thinking back to when they were kids, most people remember at least one adult who possessed this wonderful balance. Most also remember what a tremendously powerful, positive impact this person had on their lives.

> *Love and Logic teaches adults how to be*
> *strict and loving at the same time.*

Is there any other research to back this idea that positive relationships are the key? There are not enough pages in this *Journal* to list all of the findings, so let's just take a quick glimpse at a few:

- Finn (1989) found that one of the most important factors determining whether students stayed in school or dropped out was whether they felt a connection with someone at the school. In other words, those students who had relationships with teachers and other adults at school were more likely to finish.
- Kramer-Schlosser (1992) observed at-risk students achieving at a much higher level than expected when they felt their teachers knew them and cared.
- Pianta, Steinberg, and Rollins (1995) found that a warm teacher relationship played an important role in preventing children, grades kindergarten through third, from having to repeat a grade.
- All of the following have found that children have better adjustment as adults when their teachers established this type of relationship with them: Garmezy (1994); Pederson, Faucher, and Eaton (1978); Werner and Smith (1980).
- McKenna (1998), using skills taught in the book *Teaching with Love and Logic,* found significant improvement in the self-concept and behavior of a nine-year-old student significantly at risk for academic and social failure.

There remain skeptics. Some teachers argue that kids should just do what they are told—that they were hired to teach and not to build relationships with kids. This argument may have had some validity forty or fifty years ago.

Why? Back then we had the vast majority of children tricked into believing that adults could make them do anything. In other words, our culture sent consistent messages that kids had to listen to adults. At this time in history, the prime job for teachers was to teach, and they didn't have to exert much effort getting kids to do what they said.

Kids have caught on. Our culture now sends a very different type of consistent message: "Adults can't make you do anything you really don't want to."

Teachers now have a much more difficult job—gaining co-operation from students who know that their teachers hold very little power to make them do anything. Under these conditions, the only way teachers can be successful is by getting tough kids to respect, like, or even love them enough to do the things they ask.

Other skeptics argue that using relationships to get children to cooperate is manipulative. We've seen unhealthy, manipulative people try to use Love and Logic. In fact, this topic brings to mind a teacher who believed that he could get kids to do whatever he wanted by just pretending that he liked them and that he cared. He was soon convinced that Love and Logic is for the birds. His students were unruly and rude.

The good news is that kids see right through these types of schemes. Anyone who really knows challenging kids knows how fast they can see through any mask to what truly fills the heart. Luckily, Love and Logic will not work for people whose hearts are not filled with genuine care for kids.

When we at Love and Logic Institute speak of relationships, we mean two things. First, we mean that adults have high expectations, set and enforce limits, and provide a warm, caring atmosphere where the primary emphasis is placed on children's strengths. Second, we mean that adults are walking hand-in-hand with the child, growing every bit as much as the child.

When we speak of relationships, we are really talking about an honest process that affects both the child and the adult. This process evolves in predictable steps:

• The adult takes the lead by getting to know the child's interests, strengths, and concerns. The adult enters the child's world and shows that he or she values the child unconditionally.
• The child begins to feel a bond with the adult. Since this is scary, most troubled kids will act worse for just a while to test

the adult's sincerity and resolve. If the adult does not reject the child or give up, the child begins to unconsciously copy certain characteristics of the adult.

When I met my son's teacher, whom he dearly loves, I noticed that he had begun to take on some of her nonverbal gestures and speech patterns. If you want proof that this copying takes place, study couples who've been happily married for decades.

- The adult begins to see even more positives in the child and begins to bond with the child.
- The child's self-concept begins to improve. From years of research we know that positive self-concept leads to improved behavior and achievement.
- The adult realizes how much easier it is to work with the child.

What we see in this process is a reciprocal respect and liking between the adult and the child. The work "reciprocal" is key here.

Simply put, when Love and Logic talks about relationships, what it's really talking about is a process where both the child and the adult draw closer in a very genuine, nonmanipulative way. When this takes place teachers discover the joy of teaching, and children discover the joy of learning.

References

Finn, J. (1989). Withdrawing from the school. *Review of Educational Research*, 59, 117–142.

Garmezy, N. (1994). Reflections and commentary on risk, resilience, and development. In R.J. Haggerty, L. Sherrod, N. Garmezy, and M. Rutter (Eds.), *Stress, risk, and resilience in children and adolescents: Processes, mechanisms, and interventions* (pp. 1–19). New York: Cambridge University Press.

Kramer-Schlosser, L. (1992). Teacher distance and student disengagement: School lives on the margin. *Journal of Teacher Education*, 43, 128–140.

McKenna, J. (1998). Unpublished master's thesis.

Pederson, E., Faucher, T.A., and Eaton, W.W. (1978). A new perspective on the effects of first-grade teachers on children's subsequent adult status. *Harvard Educational Review*, 48, 1–31.

Pianta, R.C., Steinberg, M., and Rollins, K. (1995). The first two years of school: Teacher–child relationships and deflections in children's classroom adjustment. *Development and Psychopathology*, 7, 297–312.

Werner, E., and Smith, R. (1980). *Vulnerable but invincible*. New York: Wiley.

© 2001 Charles Fay, Ph.D.

CLINE'S CORNER

"The School Just Isn't Being Fair"
By Foster W. Cline, M.D.

VOL. 17, NO. 1

I received a letter from a mom. She was upset because the school wasn't giving her daughter credit for the homework she turned in late, and the mom thought she had a valid excuse for turning it in late.

"Shouldn't the child be given recognition for what she completes, even if she is late for a good reason?" Mom wanted to go to the school and talk to the teacher.

Maybe partial credit should have been given. Maybe not. Luckily, Love and Logic parents don't have to figure out if a teacher is unfair or if a child only *sees and feels* the situation is unfair. Both situations occur in life, and in both cases, people of character learn to cope.

Let's look at other examples of school decisions that could or could not be seen as overreactions or unfair:

"If the homework is late, you get a zero. There is no excuse for getting it in late—even if your grandmother dies or something!"

"All I did was hit Jimmy back and not even hard, after he'd been pounding on us all for days! He deserved it! It worked, and he's a lot nicer to us now. I should be given a medal! Why should I be suspended for a week for that?"

"But it was only a tiny plastic picnic knife, okay? I didn't say I was going to cut anyone's eyes or heart out or anything! Why should I be suspended for having a plastic knife on my key chain?"

"We had a pop quiz on Thursday, and anyone who missed three or more words has to write them each two hundred times! I shouldn't have to write six hundred words! That's crazy!"

"Zero tolerance" has led to some situations that appear a little crazy. One teen was suspended for a pocketknife in the glove box of her car, and she was the one who reported it! Life is, as the old saying goes, unfair.

But somehow, more than in the past, we have become a nation of victims. We look for unfairness. Why is this? I think it is because there is too much rescuing going on.

For example, politicians feed on unfairness. Look at the headlines, and you will see politician after politician capitalizing on people's feelings of victimization. As politicians and parents search for victims to rescue, they not only encourage victimhood, they actually lower the ability of the kids (and the whole population) to cope.

Love and Logic parents help their kids cope by empathizing with their feelings (regardless of the "merit" of the feelings):

You are so lucky when the school does things that seem unfair or don't make sense to you. Because you know what, Joyce, you're growing up into a world where a lot of things don't make very good sense—and may at times be downright unfair.

Lucky for you, you're getting to learn how to cope with those actions and your feelings now. You can learn to react thoughtfully when you are just a kid! Imagine that! You're going to have a real jump on the poor guys that only learn how to handle things that seem unfair when they are adults.

There are many ways kids can learn to handle things that seem or actually are unfair:

- They can be encouraged to talk to school authorities themselves.
- They can become articulate by writing an article in the school paper or letting others know their ideas in another way.

- They can be encouraged to make an end-run and appeal to a higher authority.
- They can be helped to cope with their feelings and come up with alternative solutions.
- They can look into AdvancedAcademics.com and other wonderful education alternatives on the Internet.
- They can check out comparable situations in other schools and at metro colleges.
- They can cope by simply enduring a semester and realizing better times are ahead.

There is no end to ways that kids can be taught to cope with feelings and develop quality responses as long as their parents don't rescue them.

Almost all truly great leaders have cut their teeth on handling adversity and tough times—not by being rescued from them. (However, when a child is absolutely incapable of coping, and the child knows that we know they cannot cope, then there is nothing lost by rescuing them. Rescuing gives the message of inability to cope, and if that's the case with our special needs child, then rescue.)

Thoughtful Americans may wonder about the results of institutionalized victimhood so obvious all across America—manifested everywhere by burgeoning governmental programs and hovering, overprotective parents. Overprotection and rescue wreak havoc by decreasing the ability to cope. A major manifestation of inability to cope is rage, a compound emotion of anger, frustration, and helplessness. Everywhere one looks, one sees the prevalence of increasing rage.

"Air rage" is reported to have increased 800 percent in the last two years. Organizations such as Sky Rage are dedicated to helping flight attendants and passengers cope with the increasing dangers of flying. Articles in national magazines decry "desk rage."

One could make the argument that as government and parental protection becomes ubiquitous, we are developing a society filled with individuals who feel entitled, unable to cope, and easily frustrated when not rescued. These individuals are increasingly expressing their feelings of inadequacy with outbursts of rage.

© 2001 Foster W. Cline, M.D.

What an Inconvenience
By Jim Fay
VOL. 17, NO. 2

Are effective consequences those that hurt kids, or are they the ones that leave them feeling inconvenienced and uncomfortable? If you answered "inconvenienced," you are on the right track for being a Love and Logic parent or teacher.

Love and Logic consequences are never designed to leave kids either hurt or feeling angry toward the adults. Inconvenience does a great job of causing kids to think about their mistakes over a longer period of time. The result is that they start thinking, "I'm not sure I want to do that again."

A good friend recently related a story in which her son had the misfortune of wrecking his car. This is a good kid. What he did was probably more out of inexperience than for any other reason.

But as Mom said to him, "Todd, this is such a gift for you. Nobody got hurt. And I'm sure you've learned a great deal about how cars perform on ice and snow."

To me she said, "Dad and I know that we're doing the right thing, but Jim, I've got to tell you it takes a lot of courage to watch the inconvenience he has created for himself. It's also not always easy to remember that his anger is directed more at the situation than it is at us.

"Todd has been without a car for two months. He has been catching rides with his friends. We give him rides when we can, and he stays home more now than before.

"He also thinks we are being unfair for not letting him use our cars or replacing his. The fact that his friends' parents replace cars every time they get wrecked doesn't make it any easier. He's yet to figure out that the reason his friend drives so wildly has something to do with his not having to worry about where the next car comes from.

"Dad and I believe that holding Todd responsible for this accident may save his life in the future. But I'm sure he will only appreciate that when he has kids of his own."

Mom went on to tell how Todd had to go to work to replace the car and to raise the money for his traffic ticket and increased insurance rates.

"Recently he had no way to get to work and decided that he would just have to call a cab. At first we wanted to tell him he couldn't order a cab. But then we got to thinking that he was spending his own money and that another great lesson might just be on its way, so we decided to stay out of his decision.

"He had to wait forty-five minutes for the cab to arrive. This made him all the more upset."

Mom had a twinkle in her eye as she said, "The longer he waited, the more upset he became. Dad and I stayed out of his way as he stormed around impatiently complaining about how long it was taking for the cab to arrive.

"When he came home that night the first thing he said was, 'Boy, I'm never doing that again! I had to wait for that guy for forty-five minutes and then he charged me forty dollars to take me to work. I lost money today! I'm never going through that again!'"

Upon hearing this story I couldn't help but think about how much courage it took for Todd's parents to do the right thing. It would have been so much easier for them to relieve their son's inconvenience.

How tempting it must have been for them to think that rescuing Todd would be an okay thing to do, since he is usually responsible.

Then Mom's words came back to me: "Todd, this is such a gift for you. Nobody was hurt, and you've learned so much."

I asked Mom about her courage and she answered, "I love Todd. I think holding him accountable may save his life someday. I know that he will be a safe driver as a result.

"I worry, though, about his friend whose parents bail him out of every misdeed. The odds for his dying because of wild driving are far greater than they need to be."

Do these parents deserve a medal or what? No, they don't need a medal. They're going to have a far greater reward. They are raising a youngster who does not see them as the source of his problems.

Todd is becoming a young man who is equipped to live in a world full of decisions and consequences.

© 2001 Jim Fay

Solving the Dependent Learner Problem: Mornings May Be More Important Than You Think!
By Charles Fay, Ph.D.

VOL. 17, No. 2

"I need help."

"This is too hard."

"I can't do this by myself."

Have these words ever flown from the lips of your kids as they sit in front of homework? If you're a teacher, have you heard these sad sentences muttered over and over again in your classroom?

In my travels across the country, I hear thousands of parents and educators describe the same unfortunate problem—bright kids who seem unable to complete academic assignments without constant guidance from an adult.

I refer to these youngsters as "dependent learners." Sadly, there are plenty of these kids. The following scenario, between a bright child and a caring adult, unfolds multiple times daily in classrooms and homes across our great nation:

CHILD: (calls across room) "I don't get it. This problem's too hard. I need help."

ADULT: (walks over to child) "What's the first step I showed you earlier?"

CHILD: (shrugging shoulders) "I don't know."

ADULT: (patiently) "Do you remember? Cross-multiply these numbers, here."

CHILD: (begins to work as adult stands close by)

ADULT: "Great! You have it!" (walks away from child)

CHILD: (37.5 seconds later begins to stare into the distance)

ADULT: (walks over) "What's wrong?"

CHILD: "Um, I got these numbers, but what do I do now?"

ADULT: (still trying to be patient) "Do you remember what I showed you earlier? The second step is to add these numbers, here."

CHILD: (begins working as the adult stands close by)

ADULT: (walks away)

CHILD: (raises hand after 37.5 seconds) "I'm stuck."

And the saga continues ...

In this example, we have a bright child who is very capable of working independently. We also have a smart, caring, and very patient adult. So what's the problem?

This child believes that he or she cannot learn or perform without constant reminders and reassurance. As time goes by, as schoolwork gets harder and teachers expect greater levels of independence, this child will face bigger and bigger problems.

Where do the primary roots of this problem lie? Not with teachers, and not with schools! The more experience I have with children, their families, and their schools, the more I've seen that the seeds of the dependent learner problem are planted during the third and fourth years of life—when well-meaning parents give too many reminders and do too much nagging.

If you've fallen into the habit of giving too many reminders and warnings, don't beat yourself up! Parents make this mistake out of great love for their children.

Let's take a look at an all-too-common morning in America:

PARENT: (calling from another room) "Julie? Are you done getting dressed yet?"

CHILD: (silence)

PARENT: (walks in child's room to see this four-year-old playing instead of getting dressed) "This is the third time I've asked you to get going! What is going on here?"

CHILD: "Don't know."

PARENT: (putting the child's shirt and shoes on) "You are old enough to get ready! Why does it take you so long?"

CHILD: "Don't know."

Ten minutes later ...

PARENT: (quite frustrated by now) "If you make me late again, I'm going to be really mad. Aren't you done with breakfast yet? I told you to eat five minutes ago."

CHILD: (whining) "But I don't like it ... It's cold."

Ten minutes later ...

PARENT: (angry) "You still haven't eaten? Now we are late! Where is your coat? This is the third time I've told you to get your coat. Where did you put it?"

CHILD: "Don't know."

PARENT: "Here it is. Now put it on and let's go."

CHILD: (still whining) "But I'm hungry."

What is this child learning? Simply put, she's being conditioned to believe the following:

1. I can't remember what I've been told.
2. I need someone to tell me what to do.
3. I need someone to guide me through my life, one step at a time.
4. If I forget, somebody will do it for me.

Is there a connection between how parents handle mornings during the early years of life and how kids approach learning later in school? Absolutely!

Just think of the massive amount of conditioning that can take place before a child ever walks into the kindergarten classroom. Let's see ... 365 days a year multiplied by 3 (the number of years between ages three and six) ... that's 1,095 separate morning training sessions! If we include bedtimes, the number doubles to a staggering 2,190!

When parents handle mornings and bedtimes well, their kids get more than 2,000 opportunities to look at themselves and say, "Look at me! I can do this without being reminded or nagged. I've got what it takes!"

The glory here is that kids who think this at age four are very likely to think it again—when they're ten and their teachers hand them assignments to complete.

What's the good news? It's never too late to turn things around for yourself and your kids. The key is to start by showing your youngsters that they can handle getting ready to leave the house with a minimum of assistance from you.

Listed below are steps for making this happen with children of all ages.

Step 1: Don't fight unnecessary battles over clothes, hair, etc.
Don't sweat the small stuff! Find clothes that match your child's abilities.

My son had a horrible time with buttons and zippers when he was younger. Instead of battling over this issue, we bought about six different sweatshirt and sweat-pant combinations. All he had to do was pull the pants up and pull the shirt down.

Is it just me, or do other parents feel tempted to become fashion designers for their kids? I often ask, "In twenty years or so, will I look back and wish my child had been better dressed in school?" Absolutely not!

It's also helpful to remember that most teachers do not subtract points for messy hair or mismatched clothing. When kids get older, they begin to experiment with how they like to dress, how to style their hair, and how they want to look. This is healthy. By the time they become teenagers, this experimentation can lead to some rather shocking looks! Avoid battles over clothing and hair at all costs. Just take lots of pictures so you can blackmail your kids when they grow up and have their own families!

If we avoid fights over these issues, our children will eventually grow out of this phase. If we do battle, they will spend the rest of their lives trying to upset and shock us with their looks and their actions.

Step 2: Brainwash yourself.

Parents often comment that they know the "right" thing to do but find it hard to do when they feel stressed, hurried, or angry. Do yourself and your kids a favor. Don't make any changes until you've come up with a magic sentence you can say to yourself—over and over—when you feel like nagging or reminding.

I use this one: "Keep your mouth shut ... keep your mouth shut ... keep your mouth shut ..." This silent sentence helps me remember my goal. Find one that works well for you, and practice it.

It's also very helpful to listen to our audiocassette *Avoiding Power Struggles with Kids*. Listen to this tape over and over.

Step 3: Guide your child in making a "to do" list for mornings, and do some practice sessions.

When times are relaxed, sit down with your child and say something like, "You're old enough now to get ready in the morning by yourself. So I don't have to remind or nag you, I'd like you to make a list of the things you will need to do each morning. What are they?"

Very young children can have fun by drawing and coloring pictures symbolizing what they need to remember. For example, a toothbrush means "brush my teeth," a coat means "get my coat," a pair of shoes means "put my shoes on," etc. When this list is completed, have your child post it someplace where he or she can look at it each morning.

The smartest parents even do some practice sessions with their younger kids. When times are calm, and nobody is in a hurry, they make a fun game out of pretending it's time to get ready and teaching their kids how to do it. For kids seven and older, show them how to set their own alarm clock.

Step 4: Remember to share the control.
Wise parents never forget to give plenty of small choices like the following:

> "Will you be getting dressed first or eating first?"
> "Do you want milk or juice?"
> "Are you going to wear this blue shirt or this red one?"

Step 5: Use three very powerful enforceable statements.

1. Replace "Hurry up" with "The car is leaving in ten minutes. Will you be going with your clothes on your body or your clothes in a bag?" With older kids and teenagers, you may experiment with this: "The bus comes between 7:30 and 7:45. Are you going to be riding it or paying someone to drive you?" (or "... paying a sitter to stay with you?")
2. Replace "Eat" with "Breakfast is served until 7:15. Get what you need to hold you until lunch."
3. Replace "Brush your teeth" with "We give treats to kids who protect their teeth by brushing."

Of course, be prepared to back these statements with lots of empathy and solid consequences. This means that your child may need to get dressed in the car, pay a baby-sitter with toys, go without breakfast, or do without treats for a while. Simply put, enforceable statements mean nothing unless we follow through.

Step 6: Enjoy a more responsible, independent child.
At one of my Love and Logic conferences for educators, a school principal approached me, grinned ear-to-ear, and said, "One of the parents at my school called yesterday and said he'd been to your class."

Over and over his eight-year-old would dawdle and miss the bus. Then Dad would be late for work due to driving the boy to school.

"I guess they used your tips. They even planned to have him pay a baby-sitter if he didn't get ready in time."

"I bet he was shocked when the baby-sitter arrived!" I interrupted.

"That's the funny part," he continued. "When Dad gave him the choice and said, 'The bus comes by at 7:50. Are you going to school or paying a baby-sitter?' the kid jumped up and started scrambling around, looking for his socks and shoes.

"Guess the parents were even more shocked when he flew out of the house in time for the bus! They never had to call the baby-sitter."

Why did this child respond the way he did? There are at least two reasons. First, when his parents shared control through choices and enforceable statements, he no longer had to hoard it by moving slowly.

Second, he probably noticed how much less his parents were worrying about him getting ready on time. Something very fascinating often happens as a result:

The less we *worry about a child's responsibilities,*
the more they *have to.*

Every time I hear a story like this, it warms my heart. Why? Every time a child learns to do something independently, he or she is better prepared for school—and years later for work. Every time a child succeeds like this, he or she feels better about him- or herself. And every time a parent takes positive action, the world becomes a better place.

© 2001 Charles Fay, Ph.D.

"What Shall We Do with This Teen?"
By Foster W. Cline, M.D.
VOL. 17, NO. 2

I often get letters from parents saying something like this:

You probably don't remember me, but we met at a conference in ...
Our son has been caught smoking marijuana and was suspended

from the football team for a short period of time. He seemed to have learned his lesson and was seemingly doing well.

We've since found out he had been skipping out of basketball games for half an hour to an hour at a time with a group of boys. We told him he would not be able to stay for varsity games (he plays JV basketball), since we could not trust him to be where he was supposed to be.

Last week we caught him smoking pot in his bedroom. We turned him in to the police and they have sent him to a drug diversion program.

It just seems like the offenses keep piling up; he is getting more defiant and distant. He is sixteen and a half and, from our experience with our older adopted daughter, we know this is a rough age. What we wonder is, if he is setting this up so he can be angry and justify leaving at seventeen.

Our oldest adopted daughter did that. Is there a way to defuse the situation? We feel like there must be a better way than piling up consequence upon consequence, but what do we do about the trust issue?

As soon as he is allowed to go we will be facing those same issues again. We try hard to use natural consequences and it seems that not having the privilege of going addresses the fact that we can't trust him. The drug problem is being handled by the police.

Do you have any suggestions as to a better way to handle his refusal to keep what seems like a pretty easy, logical rule?

Answer

Such questions are difficult, and the parents and the teens are often in pain. Many parents learn through heartbreak that everyone, for better or worse, does have free will.

I usually suggest in these heartbreaking situations that parents write a letter and set a good example by taking care of themselves. It may be that their teen can't say no to peers, but parents can pave the way by demonstrating to teens that they do, beyond a shadow of a doubt, take good care of themselves.

This taking good care of yourself is the message of Alanon and the message that keeps most people out of codependent situations.

The letter goes something like this:

Dear Bob,

We thought it best to write to you, and ask for your written response, as thoughts in writing are more clear and don't get mixed up with body posture or tone of voice, and purity of the thought shines through.

Main point: We love you.

Second, we realize that, in our love for you we have perhaps been overinvolved in your successes and failures. All of us must live our own lives, make our own decisions, decide who we want to be around or live with, whether or not we want an education, and whether or not we are in trouble with the law.

So we opt out of messing around in your life.

Bob, you are an adult. By that, I mean that from now on your decisions about drug use, school, friends, and activities are up to you. Those things are your business. And even if they were our business, we couldn't control them. Sorry we ever thought about trying!

*So from now on, we are only going to be concerned about the issues that affect us **directly**. That is, how people treat us, how honest they are, whether or not people are respectful to us—all the things that you, too, have to decide for yourself.*

Dad and I will do our best to be respectful, responsible, and fun to be around. We won't use drugs in your presence and we will never bring drugs onto your property—no sense losing a home or apartment because someone else brings drugs on it. If anyone else ever does bring drugs to your apartment, we hope you call the cops before you lose it.

If you choose to live here, we expect you to be respectful and fun to be around—just what your wife would expect. No big deal, but essential for people who live together.

Anyway, we'll tell you where we are, and when we expect to be home. That's just common courtesy. We expect the same from you. We'll be honest with you, but don't pry directly into our lives. We expect you to be honest with us, and we won't pry directly into yours.

If we are ever locked up, or need a lawyer, we won't call you. We'll have to take care of those kinds of problems ourselves.

The same goes for you. No matter what kind of problem you get into, there are always public defenders that might be able to help you. But don't depend on them. Most are young, inexperienced, and don't work too hard for kids.

So, dear son, make decisions that you think best for you. But be honest with us. And we'll let you know where we are.

We know that with your values, you don't want to feel like you are freeloading off of us. Therefore, we want you to know for sure that you are always welcome to live here, and we'll support you as long as you are preparing for life.

When you show by your actions, or by grades below passing, that school is no longer important for you, then we'll understand that you know that you are prepared to deal with life and our support will naturally not be needed.

At that point, you can choose anywhere you would like to live or pay us $400 per month, in advance, to live here. When we are old, if we ever need to live with you, we will do the same.

That's about it. Hope it sounds super fair and you can feel freer to make your own decisions about your own life now that you are an adult. Our love will follow you wherever your life's path takes you or wherever you end up living. (Cellblock 44, Ward 9, #2456792. Just kidding—but you never know.)

Therefore, dear son, if you agree to these "live and let live" rules, and choose to continue to live here, please sign below within the next three business days.

People who choose to live at the following address:

_____

_____

_____

1. Will be fun to be around, responsible, and respectful.

2. Will mind their own business.

3. Will let the others know where they are and when they expect to be home. People who live at this address will be honest with each other.

4. Will make the decisions they need to make about their own lives and handle the consequences.

5. Will either help with the mortgage, electricity, and water payments or be preparing for life.

6. Won't bring drugs onto these premises or engage in illegal activities on these premises.

Signatures of those who choose to live at address:

_____

_____

_____

_____

P.S. If anything here doesn't seem fair, let us know in writing and we'll give your thoughts careful consideration.

© 2001 Foster W. Cline, M.D.

"Is That You, Grandma?"

By Jim Fay

VOL. 17, NO. 3

Every available unit blocked the streets leading to the high school. Yards and yards of crime-scene tape kept spectators well away. Officers, nerves quivering, kneeled behind squad cars. Their eyes never left the entrance to the high school.

The swat team had finally arrived and was setting up. Each man was hoping not to be called upon to fire his weapon as he skillfully moved into his assigned position.

Five hours had passed since fifteen-year-old Billy took his hostage. A terrified youngster had survived all this time with a gun held to his neck. He knew that each minute that passed was possibly his last.

The police psychologist was using every skill he knew in his attempt to calm the boy who held the gun, in hopes that he could see the wisdom of giving himself up. He knew that the wrong words at this time could summon a bloody end to the standoff.

Alas, his shoulders sagged as he retreated to the safety of the command post and announced, "I don't know what else to do. I'm afraid he's so scared that I can't get him to understand the benefits of giving up the gun."

The chief of police quickly summoned his deputies to a conference with the mayor and his advisers. It seemed that they had only one choice left, and not one person wanted to be the one to voice it.

Finally the chief said, "I know that our only choice is to ask the swat team to do a surgical removal of the boy with the gun. It's possible that a well-placed shot will take him out before he can fire his gun. At least we will save one boy." He was then quick to add, "But I know not one of us wants to make that decision."

The psychologist had one more idea: "Does this boy have a grandma? Sometimes kids will listen to their grandparents even when they won't listen to anyone else." A quick search located his grandma. She was living in a nursing home in that very town.

That day, ninety-year-old Grandma had her very first helicopter ride. She was helped out of the helicopter right onto the street in front of the school. The chief and his deputies were there to meet her. Anxiously they asked if she thought she could talk to Billy, her grandson.

"Of course I can talk to him. What do you think? He's my grandson. I spent of a lot of time raisin' that youngun." With that she started up the stairs toward the school, only to be stopped by the officers.

"You can't go in there yet. We have to fit you with body armor."

"I don't need no body armor. He's my grandson. You don't know nothing 'bout grandmas and their kids!" And with that she hobbled up the steps to the front door of the school.

Opening the door just a few inches, she yelled in, "Billy!"

Flabbergasted officers heard a faint reply, "That you, Grandma?"

"Yes and I'm comin' in there."

To this day I can visualize ninety-year-old Grandma waddling down the hall and marching herself right up to Billy. "Billy, you ought to be ashamed of yourself! Now you give me that gun, and give yer old grandma a hug!"

As if he were in a daze, Billy slowly handed the gun to his grandma. And with tears in his eyes he said, "Sorry, Grandma. I jus' din't know what to do. I was so scared."

Grandma turned to the officers, and with resolution said, "Take this boy somewhere so's I can give him a good talkin' to."

There was so much speculation that day. Why did Billy so readily comply with Grandma's orders? He had defied all the major authority figures who tried to deal with him during this ordeal. Grandma was obviously the most physically weak of all those, yet he responded to her like a trained seal.

Many studies in psychology give us some insights into this phenomenon. One of these studies dealt with fleas. The researchers put them in a jar. The jar was short enough that the fleas could easily jump out.

A clear glass lid was then placed over the top of the jar. Each time the fleas jumped, they bumped their heads on the glass. After a period of time the glass was removed. Lo and behold, from that time on the fleas could never jump out. In fact, the researchers found that the fleas could only jump to a height just slightly below the level of the glass.

The fleas did not have a problem with the strength of their legs. They had a problem with conditioning. Their brains were conditioned to believe that they could only jump to a certain height.

My seven-pound dog can jump up onto a high bed. He can also jump down easily. However, he cannot jump off the bed at night.

He believes that Shirley or I have to lift him down regardless of how important it is for him to get down.

How can this be? It's called conditioning. When he was a small puppy he slept on the bed with us. He could not get off without hurting himself. So one of us always picked him up and put him onto the floor. This happened on a repetitive basis. His brain became wired to believe that he couldn't jump off the bed in the dark.

So, you ask, "How is it that he can jump on and off the bed during daylight hours?" The answer is that he only started going into the bedroom during the daytime when he was much older, at a time when he was strong enough to jump high.

This helps us understand why Billy responded to Grandma and not to the authorities. We know that Billy's brain has been conditioned to believe that he cannot defy Grandma. These connections were made in his brain when he was small.

Grandma was raising him at this time. We can be sure that she handled discipline problems with him in a special way. She was careful to never give an order or request that she couldn't control easily.

Each time Billy saw Grandma get her way without effort, anger, or frustration, he thought to himself, "Oh, man. If she can handle me so easily, there's no way I can win a battle with her. She can handle me no matter what I do."

Before long his little brain developed hardwiring that said, "I have to do what Grandma says. She is always sweet and kind, but I know that she's the boss." Billy's brain grew to see Grandma as a very loving, yet powerful, authority figure.

Had Grandma exerted her authority with anger and frustration, Billy's brain would have been wired to believe something totally different about her role as an authority figure. His mind would have constantly said, "Well, she got her way, but it wasn't easy. If I keep trying, or if I get bigger, she won't be able to handle me."

We see many kids today who think like this. Their parents may be using the right techniques, but what success they have looks to the child like hard work. They are raising their voices, threatening, and displaying anger.

Without knowing it, these parents are conditioning their kids to think, "Well, Mom or Dad got their way this time, but it wasn't easy. Just wait till I'm a little bigger. They won't be telling me what to do."

Your own kids are going to be conditioned one way or the other. There is no neutral position on this. Love and Logic teaches us to discipline our kids without anger or frustration. Now you know why it is so important.

© 2001 Jim Fay

Toxic Birthday Parties:
Just Say "No!" to Keeping Up with the Joneses
By Charles Fay, Ph.D.

VOL. 17, No. 3

Is it just me, or have children's birthday parties gotten out of hand? Am I big meanie, or does it seem a bit outrageous to invite the entire kindergarten class, hire a caterer, and cap off the event with a trip to the amusement park?

I learned of this party during one of my recent consulting trips. It left me wondering a lot of things. What will this kid's sixteenth birthday party look like? Is this approach setting her up for being pretty spoiled and demanding as she ages? How does one keep track of twenty excited little bodies at an amusement park? Was the cotton candy included? Why wasn't I invited to parties like this when I was a kid?

Am I really just too antimaterialistic? Am I consumerism-impaired? Or are kids getting too much stuff these days?

At a party we recently survived, a small child was lost for almost an hour. Rescue teams were called in, search dogs went to work, and he was eventually found, still breathing under the massive toys he'd received from all his friends. All's well that ends well!

I know I probably sound old-fashioned, but does it seem like a bad birthday party idea to send your ten-year-old daughter and six of her friends to the Britney Spears concert ... without supervision? Nothing against Britney—or even groups like INSTYNK—it's just that old "parental supervision hang-up" I have. Another great story ... that I wish weren't true.

Setting aside the joking—and the sarcasm—I worry greatly for the many children in this great nation whose parents send unhealthy, damaging messages by the way they handle birthday parties. What type of an impact might this be having on our youth?

Consider the following: Are we elevating the threshold for what children view as exciting or fun? How can anything compare to the amusement park with your entire class, a Mount Everest–like pile of toys, or a Britney concert without your Neanderthal parents?

Have times ever changed! I remember getting really excited when I had two friends over for my seventh birthday. We gorged on those sugar-filled straws (Pixie Stix), and we ran around the yard like wild animals. It was great!

I feel sad for kids who are raised to need massive amounts of excitement. For them, life soon feels pretty dull. Are we sending the message that the number of friends one has is more important than their quality? I've known many adults over the years who are the loneliest people in the world. Why are they so lonely? Simply because they have so many friends that they really have none.

Do these type of parties contribute to the "entitlement epidemic"? Might we be placing an unhealthy emphasis on what people can give instead of the quality of close, sincere human relationships?

I can remember as a child all of the big and wise people in my life teaching me more or less the same thing: Value people for their kindness, their love, and their honesty—not the material things they can give you, the clothes they wear, the cars they drive, etc. I was pretty lucky to have these "big and wise" people.

Does all of this make it harder for really responsible parents who won't, or simply can't, keep up with the Joneses?

Talking with a friend of mine, we pondered these thoughts. Sharing my woes, she said, "Yeah! And it gets to the point where I'm spending so much time running around looking for gifts, planning events, and worrying about money that I'm too stressed out to be the kind of mother I'd like to be.

"Then I even find myself feeling resentful toward some of the other parents. In my neighborhood, it seems like the least responsible of them set the 'gold standard' for gifts and parties. Now it's like a snowball. The parties are getting bigger and bigger as everyone tries to keep up with the last one."

What's more important? Is it more important to keep up with the Joneses or to teach our kids healthy values regarding relationships? And which kids are going to be more likely to take good care of their parents when they become elderly and frail?

Will it be the kids who've learned that people are important only as long as they can be exciting and produce gifts? Or will it be those who've learned that love, kindness, and character are the most valuable gifts of all?

Give yourself and your kids a break! The next time you're planning a birthday party, remember what kids want and need the very most—the closeness and love of their parents. Most people find it next to impossible to be close and loving when they're trying to orchestrate a complex party for their kids. Instead, take good care of yourself by following some guidelines:

- Keep it simple.
- Don't invite the entire town. Two close friends is better than twenty distant ones.
- On the invitations write, "No gifts please."
- Have brief talks with your child about why friends are more important than toys.
- Get lots of Pixie Stix.

© *2001 Charles Fay, Ph.D.*

Helping Kids Cope with Tragedy:
What to Say to Help Them Feel Safe and Secure
By Charles Fay, Ph.D.

VOL. 17, NO. 3

At a difficult time like this in our nation's history [after the September 11, 2001, terrorist attacks], parents all over this country—and the world—are wondering, "What do I tell my kids about this? What do I do?"

Children have an incredible capacity for strength, and parents can play a powerful role in helping their children cope with horribly difficult events. Here are some practical guidelines:

1. Be honest about your emotions while modeling strength.

Our children will cope only as well as we do. Children who see their parents overwhelmed with anxiety, fear, and grief also will become overwhelmed. On the other hand, kids will not have an opportunity to learn healthy expression of feelings if parents stuff their feelings inside.

The key is being honest about your emotions while showing that your family remains strong. For example, you might give your child a hug and say:

This is a very sad thing. Sometimes I feel like crying about it. It also makes me mad. But I know that we will be okay ... because we are strong.

2. Limit your child's exposure to media coverage of the event.

Turn the television and radio off when your kids are in the room. Repeated exposure to the visual and spoken images of the tragedy will create more anxiety and fear. Younger children who don't understand that the scenes are being replayed often believe the actual events keep happening over and over.

3. Give them the facts about the event.

Don't try to keep the tragedy a secret! First, it's simply impossible to do. Second, humans create information when they lack it. When children get bits and pieces of bad news, they "fill in the blanks" with their imagination. Typically their fears, or rumors that float about at school, produce more anxiety than the truth.

Children, even as young as two, may need you to lay out the facts about the event. Tell them the basics, while leaving out the more sensitive details. Remember, your tone of voice must communicate compassion *and* strength.

4. Listen, listen, listen.
There is nothing more powerful than an open ear, heartfelt understanding, and a warm hug.

5. Let them know that they are safe.
Our children need to hear about the thousands and thousands of wonderful people who are working day and night to keep us safe. Despite any fears or doubts we may have, our kids need to hear that they are safe.

Make your reassurance short and to the point. When parents spend too much time, too many words, and too many emotions trying to reassure kids that they are safe, it backfires. Your message will be more powerful and believable if it is very brief and businesslike:

There are thousands of people working to keep everyone safe. We are going to be okay. Have a good day at school. I love you.

6. To the greatest extent possible, maintain daily routines.
Daily routines give all of us a sense of predictability, control, and safety. When we stick with them, we also communicate to our youngsters that we are strong enough to keep going ... and they are, too.

7. Involve them in helping others.
There are few things more therapeutic than helping others. Even actions that may seem small, like writing letters of support or sending a box of food to rescue workers, can mean a great deal.

• • •

An elementary school principal who followed these tips voiced amazement at how they work. "I can't believe how well our school dealt with this yesterday. The teachers were calm, and so were the kids. Everyone is very saddened, but we are going to make it through!"

• • •

One last thought: Following these guidelines can help, but it is just as important to take good care of yourself. The healthier you are, the healthier your kids will be.

© *2001 Charles Fay, Ph.D.*

CLINE'S CORNER

Keep Your Options Open: Don't Give Warnings
By Foster W. Cline, M.D.
VOL. 17, No. 3

Mankind has a tendency to push the limits. It doesn't matter whether the perceived limits are the heights of Everest, the depths of the ocean, the vastness of outer space, or a mother's "No." Mankind, children included, wants to go as far as it can.

The problem with pushing the limits, of course, is that one can push too far. The pulsating thrill and excitement of walking the edge can quickly turn into the anguish of the fall when one goes over the precipice.

However, one can be much braver when pushing the limits if one knows there are always warnings before the consequences fall. When there has been a short storm at sea, is it safe to walk the beaches if a tsunami has pulled all the water out? The yawning beach is warning you to keep away.

On the other hand, geologists feel free to walk the volcano if there have been no pre-eruption tremors.

Moms and dads often provide pre-eruption tremors: "Hey, guys, if this continues, you are going to have to ..." Or, "If you guys don't stop this, I'm going to have to ..." In fact, the pre-eruption tremors can be labeled, numbered, packaged, and delivered: "That's once ... that's twice." Or, "One ... two ..."

What a joy it is to know ahead of time exactly how far the limits can be pushed. When Mom and Dad always give warnings before imposing consequences, it is as if one could drive, always being sure the car would say, "One more mile per hour and you'll be stopped by the cops on this section of the highway."

How fast would you drive? Would we pay attention to the speed limit? Not on your life! We'd whip down the road until the car said, "One more mile per hour and you'll be stopped by the cop on this section of the highway."

Rules don't matter if there are always warnings before the consequence occurs.

Thus, parents might have rules such as no fighting in the house, no running in the house, no hassling your little brother, etc. These rules are worthless as the parental tonsils they pass through if warnings are given. "If you guys don't quiet down, I'm gonna ask you to go to your rooms."

To ensure compliance with a rule, consequences must occur without warning.

Wise is the parent who, without warning, says, "Guys, your (hassle, language, pouting) at the table is upsetting. You need to eat on the drier." (Driers are quite accepting, as they have no ears to be hassled, and even enjoy the company of pouting children.)

Wise is the parent who says, "John, your movement through the house is hassling my eyeballs. Take yourself outside." And when the child who pushed the limits says, "I wasn't running, I was hopping," the wise parent says lovingly, and with empathy, "I know, but whatever it was, it was hassling my eyeballs—bye."

There is another Love and Logic paradox:

When children don't expect warnings, it keeps the options open.

Parents who always give warnings can't mean business. If they "ticket" the "speeding" child, they get nothing but resentment, just as all of us would feel resentful and rebellious if we expected a warning for speeding and the cop actually gave a ticket.

However, most of us, when stopped after speeding, know we will get a ticket.

It's the knowledge of the almost certain consequences that allows the merciful authority to garner gratefulness and respect when a warning is given.
When the cop says, "Dr. Cline, you were going ten miles over the speed limit, but I'm going to give you a warning this time," I drool out of sheer gratefulness on the sill of the rolled-down driver's-side window. I think the cop is one of the nicest guys I've ever met.

Yet if such warnings are rare, I'll accept the ticket next time without massive resentment. If the warning was expected, and I get a ticket, there is massive resentment.

So wise parents consequence children without warning, and they never say something really maladroit, like, "Am I going to have to ... ?"

Wise parents never let a controlling child know he or she has forced them into making decisions they'd rather not make.
But that's another Love and Logic article.

© 2001 Foster W. Cline, M.D.

"Boy, Did I Learn My Lesson"
By Jim Fay
VOL. 17, NO. 4

Do we ever grow up to the point where consequences fail to serve as the best teacher? Nope. The combination of choices, mistakes, and consequences continues to be our best teacher throughout our lives.

I learned this so well back in my early days as a consultant. I used to spend my weekends flying back and forth to New York to give presentations to teachers. These presentations were all about holding kids accountable for their actions as a way of preparing them for the real world of choices, mistakes, and consequences.

I left my school each Friday evening and flew to New York. This gave me a chance to teach on Saturday and Sunday, catch the late flight back to Denver, and arrive back to my principal job on Monday without anyone knowing that I had been gone. Life was good.

My usual routine was to have someone drive me back and forth to the conferences. Not being the driver, I didn't pay a lot of attention to directions, but over a period of time I developed a general idea about how to find Kennedy Airport. Other people were responsible for everything except my speaking responsibilities. I only had to concentrate on what I love best—dealing with the audiences. Life was good.

One Sunday, after the seminar was over, the conference planner came to me with a special request. "Jim, we have an extra rental car that needs to be dropped off at Budget Rent-a-Car. It's located at Kennedy International Airport. Can you drive it back for us since you're going there anyway?"

"Sure. No problem," I said. "I've been there many times. I'll be glad to do it for you."

I failed to think that there is a lot of difference between driving to a place and just riding there. As riders, we tend not to be as aware of the directions as drivers need to be.

"Great. Here is a set of directions to Kennedy. Maybe you'll want to take them along," warned to conference planner.

"No, I don't need them," was my confident reply. "I've been there many times."

As you can guess, I left the instructions at the hotel while I boldly struck out for Kennedy. In no time at all, I was wishing that I had the instructions. I was lost. The roads looked like massive strands of spaghetti. The prospects for finding the airport were fading fast.

I grew up in Denver. Directions were easy. Look for the mountains. They are on the west side. Easy.

I discovered something interesting that day. You can't see the Rocky Mountains from Long Island. A heavy cloud cover made it impossible for me to use the sun for directions. I was really, really lost. Life was no longer good.

I thought about asking for directions, but decided against it based upon the neighborhood I was driving through. I figured that I would run out of gas before I found my way. My mind started talking to me: "I hope that the cops find me before the gang-bangers."

I looked up just in time to see a road sign pointing to Kennedy Airport. Almost by accident I was finding my way. Now all I had to do was find the Budget Rent-a-Car. Three different times I spotted it, but it was always on the wrong side of the road beyond a service road and behind a fence. I couldn't get there.

I made a great discovery that day. Did you know that rental cars can go over curbs a lot better than your personal car? They also go the wrong way on one-way streets. I found my own way to the rental agency. The van delivered me to United Airlines just in time to miss my flight.

Racing up to the agent, I said one of the more stupid things I've said in my life: "Sorry I missed your flight."

"No problem," said the agent.

"Wait a minute. I know what that means. I teach parents to say that. It means no problem for you, big problem for me. I have to get back to work in the morning. My superintendent is going to know that I was gone and he's going to be upset that I'm doing all this traveling."

"How about sleeping on the plane. Can you do that?" asked the agent.

"No. I can't. I can't sleep sitting up."

"What a bummer," he empathized. "But if you don't mind sitting up all night, and if you don't mind riding on three different airplanes, I think I can get you back by 5:30."

"Is that in the morning? I need to get back in the morning."

"Yes. That's in the morning."

That night I got to see the Detroit airport. I got to see the Chicago airport. And I got to see the Denver airport. The day was starting to dawn when I arrived home. I had worked all day, been lost, and sat up all night. I was exhausted.

That's when I made another bad decision. "I think I'll go to bed for an hour and then go to work." You know what a bad decision that was. I was totally wiped out when I got to my office. If I hadn't been able to go into my office, shut out the world, and claim that I was in conference—I wouldn't have made it through the day.

While sitting in my office, hurting from a series of bad decisions, I finally made a good one. "Okay," I thought. "I learned a great lesson last night. I guess we never lose the opportunity to learn from our bad decisions and the consequences. No more rental cars for me. If people want me to present, they can drive me around. If they miss the plane, I'll be the one to say, 'No problem. I'll charge for my time and a hotel room.' I'm not going to get hurt like this again."

I didn't come to this decision easily. Being human, I first looked to others as the source of my problem. I needed someone to blame. If the United agent had given me a lecture, I could have focused upon him as the source of my problem. But no. He was so nice. All he could say was, "No problem. What a bummer. I can help."

With nobody to blame, I had to look at myself as the source of my problem. That forced me to look to myself for the source of a solution.

The United agent gave me a great reminder about how we work with kids to teach responsibility. Lock in the empathy before providing the consequence. Anger and lectures let people off the hook. Empathy and consequences hold people accountable for their actions.

© 2002 Jim Fay

Getting Kids Up in the Morning
By Foster W. Cline, M.D.

VOL. 17, NO. 4

Recently I received a question from a mom asking, "How do I get my adolescent up in the morning?" The problem shows in asking the question! Asking how to get an adolescent out of bed is very much like wondering, "How do I get my spouse out of bed in the morning?" The problem is a "meta problem"; that is, it is symbolic of something far deeper going wrong.

Adolescents need their sleep. Lots of teens play late and sleep later. Their bodies need a lot of sleep. Many are constantly engaged in high-energy undertakings: extreme dating, extreme skiing, extreme motorcycling, etc. They're up early for school. In fact, adolescence is one of the busiest times of life. During these years, a lot of sleep is necessary. So teens sleep late whenever they can on weekends. They often hate getting up. With parents, it's different. As we grow older, our need for sleep lessens. So, adolescents not *wanting* to get up in the morning is normal and understandable, but when it takes parental energy to get them rousted out, the family has real problems.

Obviously, a neurologically intact teen who needs his or her parents to get him or her up in the morning rules the roost. Such a teen will probably be ungrateful for this wake-up valet service, snarky much of the time, and disrespectful in general. Here again, the problem is not how to get the kid rousted out, but how to handle a teen who rules the roost and is likely disrespectful and irresponsible. In such a situation, you may happen to be a parent who is getting your teen up in the morning simply as part of a pattern of making sure they do their homework, get dressed for school, and don't cut classes.

An absolute unwillingness to get up in the morning in a previously responsive child is almost always a sign of real problems. Teen onset of a major mental illness, either schizophrenia or bipolar (manic-depressive) problems, shows up in a reversed wake/

sleep cycle in which children are up all night and asleep all day. Usually though, getting the child up in the morning is the least of the parent's problems, as the child increasingly manifests crazy or irresponsible behavior.

Adolescents may use reversed wake/sleep patterns as a conscious or unconscious way of avoiding their parents. Jerry, the son in a family I recently saw, owed his parents money, and communication with his parents was often angry and conflicted. After communication and family relationships were straightened, everyone saw his prior sleep patterns as a way of avoiding issues.

Finally, cannabis or marijuana causes an extreme lack of motivation. It is called the amotivational syndrome. With these teens, there is no real excitement about getting up, getting moving, and achieving. People of any age with no motivation enjoy playing beached whale and spending time in bed or in front of the TV. These parents, and the teen, too, of course, have problems far deeper than simply sleeping late and not getting up.

So, noting all the above, and whether it is a serious problem or not, it is simply *not* normal, after the age of kindergarten or so, for one person to need another person to get him or her up in the morning. The real question is not, "How do I get my kid up?" but "What is *really* going on here?"

Naturally, special needs kids are a different story, and many with severe cognitive deficits may need more structure. But even with these special children, needing to get them up in the morning is probably a danger sign of parents enabling dysfunctional behavior.

Do read, enjoy, and learn from *Parenting Teens with Love and Logic*. It's never too late to start turning things around.

© 2002 Foster W. Cline, M.D.

VOLUME

18

How Do You Know When They're Ready?

By Jim Fay

VOL. 18, NO. 1

You're just treating me like a baby. Of course some kids might bring drugs or beer. But you don't have to worry about me. I can handle it. I'm not a baby, you know. So what if I'm only fourteen. I'm a very mature fourteen-year-old. You can't keep treating me like I'm a baby!

Betty's daughter wants to go to a party. But this mom is not sure her daughter is ready to handle the peer pressures of drugs or alcohol. It doesn't help that Betty's little cherub keeps telling her that she's being overprotective by questioning her ability to handle the peer pressure.

Last night Mom heard the news on television about yet another teenage death due to an overdose of Ecstasy, the latest drug tempting the teens at their local high school. The front page of the local newspaper poured out a common story that strikes at the hearts of parents. The story was all about a fifteen-year-old girl from a "good home." This girl was popular, got good grades, and had a wonderful future ahead of her. But now she lies on a slab in the morgue. The dreams of her parents lie shattered with her.

How could this happen. She didn't run with a bunch of bad kids. Her friends all had the best of everything and were part of the "in crowd." The newspaper article posed the question, "Why would kids like this need to be messing with drugs?" Indeed, why can't these kids say no to drugs?

Needless to say, Betty has this on her mind at the same time her daughter is demanding to know why she can't go to the next party. Mom is torn. Part of her thinks that she's done a good job of teaching her kids about the danger of drugs and the importance of resisting peer pressure. And then a riveting thought hits her: "I have trouble saying no to my own friends. I often give in to their requests even when I don't want to. If I have trouble saying no, how is my teenager supposed to do any better?"

Love and Logic to the Rescue

Betty can use a Love and Logic technique in situations like this. It is designed to help determine whether or not a youngster is ready to handle these kinds of situations. Applying the "What's Your Plan?" strategy will greatly add to your own peace of mind when your kids claim they can handle peer pressure and you simply don't know if they can.

It's All in the Plan

Betty could ask her daughter, "What's your plan if your friends want you to drink or do some drugs with them? I'll know that you're ready to handle these kinds of situations once you have a good plan. And that means that you can go to the party."

Remember that kids have some great con games designed to convince us that they are mature and ready to handle what the world offers them. These "cons" are laced with things parents are hoping to hear. Unfortunately, they are only smoke screens designed to get parents to give in. A wise parent sees them for what they are, indicators that the youngster has yet to develop a real plan for resisting peer pressure.

"I'm Not Ready" Indicators

Not Ready Indicator Number One: "Oh, Mom. You know I don't do stuff like that. I'm a good kid." Beware! This youngster has not developed a plan for handling peer pressure and is trying to say what is expected.

Not Ready Indicator Number Two: "Don't you trust me? Why can't you just trust me?" Uh, oh! This is probably a manipulation to put the parent on the defensive. Many kids learn at an early age that defensive parents are more likely to give in.

Not Ready Indicator Number Three: "Oh, Mom. I just do what you told me. I just say no." Watch out! It's a rare adult who is comfortable saying no to a good friend. This kid is not ready.

Not Ready Indicator Number Four: "I'll just tell them that doing drugs is stupid." This youngster is probably not going to say this. It is very rare for a child to risk his/her standing in the peer group with this kind of statement. This statement is usually made to impress the parent only.

The "I'm Ready" Indicator

A teenager who is ready to handle the pressure usually indicates a well-thought-out plan. This teen would probably say, "You know, Mom. When a kid wants me to try drugs, I tell him that I like him and want to do things with him, but drugs really aren't my thing. And then I thank him and suggest something else we could do, like go get a pizza together."

We can all feel pretty proud of this youngster. He seems to be well prepared for peer pressure. But do kids usually come up with these social skills all on their own? Was he born with this special ability? Probably not. Most kids need some parental guidance and practice to be able to handle themselves like this. That's where parents can be a big help.

Don't assume that your kids were born into the "Lucky Genetics Club." This means that they were born with all the good looks, wisdom, skills, and techniques they will need in life. Kids need training and they need to practice. Wise parents provide both.

© 2002 Jim Fay

Easygoing Kids Need Love and Logic Too!
By Charles Fay, Ph.D.
VOL. 18, NO. 1

Have you ever noticed how some kids resist everything we say, while others seem to thrive on anticipating what we want so they can please us?

Strong-willed kids keep us honest. They quickly teach us that sloppy parenting practices, such as warnings, lectures, and threats, are about as effective as fighting a fire with gasoline. When we warn, "Eat," they put their forks down and glare defiantly at anything green on their plates. When we remind, "Do your homework," their pencils almost always keep breaking. When we threaten, "If you don't take out the trash ... ," they wait with excitement to see what type of consequence we will develop ... so they can mumble in response to it, "I don't care." These kids do us a favor. When our parenting performance begins to slip, they don't hesitate to let us know.

Easygoing kids are a different story. Unfortunately, their politeness can trick us into believing that really crummy techniques actually work. Lectures, threats, warnings, and anger seem to work with them ... at least until the hormones begin to flow. How sad! This leaves really sweet, compliant kids at risk as they enter adolescence. How?

I grew up with lots of very nice, easygoing kids. I'd been to three funerals of nice, easygoing kids by the time I graduated from high school. No child should die from a drug overdose, alcohol-related traffic accident, eating disorder, or suicide. Very sadly, many do. When it happens to easygoing kids, we all wonder, "She was such a sweet kid. We never saw it coming. How could something like this happen?"

There's a huge risk with compliant kids. There's a huge risk that, when they become teens, they'll be too compliant to resist when they hear things like, "I've only had three beers. Don't worry. There's no cops on this road."

There's also a risk that they will never develop a strong enough sense of self ... or self-concept ... to cope with the intense pressures of adolescence and young adulthood. Sexuality, unhealthy societal messages about thinness, popularity struggles, and academic stresses can become too much for someone with shaky self-esteem.

Why are compliant kids at risk? Because they give us few clues when we forget to give them enough opportunities to make decisions, make mistakes, and learn to live with the consequences of their wise ... and unwise ... choices. As Love and Logic teaches, mistakes made early in life have much smaller "price tags" than those made later.

Love and Logic also reminds us that self-esteem grows when children encounter struggles (such as mistakes) and see themselves being strong enough to live with the consequences and to solve the resulting problem. There is nothing more satisfying and reassuring than seeing oneself as capable in this way. Easygoing kids often make too few mistakes ... and have few too opportunities to experience this healthy sense of control and competence.

Love and Logic offers a powerful process for giving compliant kids ... all kids ... an opportunity to develop the decision-making skills, wisdom, and self-esteem essential for real-world survival. Fans of our approach know this process as "The Four Steps to Responsibility." Parents of very easygoing kids might be smart to get some scissors, cut out the following section of this article, and paste it on their refrigerators.

THE FOUR STEPS TO RESPONSIBILITY

1. Give plenty of opportunities to make decisions about issues that are not life-or-death and that do not create problems for others.
2. Hope and pray that your child makes plenty of mistakes when the "price tags" of these mistakes are still small.
3. Let empathy followed by logical consequences do the teaching. Avoid anger, lectures, or threats.
4. Give your child a vote of confidence by giving them plenty of opportunities to make the same decisions again.

A friend of mine has one of these easygoing kids. Since birth, little Larry has smiled most of the time, has eaten most of his vegetables, goes to bed without a fuss, and even does his chores with few or no reminders! Yes, kids like this do exist! Research tells us that some kids are born more easygoing than others.

After learning more about Love and Logic, my friend became worried about Larry. "Maybe he isn't making enough mistakes," she wondered. Motivated to give him the best, she sat down one evening and listed all of the mistakes she hoped he'd make. Her list looked something like the following:

AFFORDABLE MISTAKES FOR LARRY

Forget his lunch.

Not study for a spelling test.

Forget to take out the trash.

Waste his allowance on a cheap, breakable toy.

Forget his coat when it's cool but not too cold.

Lose his lunchbox at school and have to earn another by doing extra chores.

Fail to eat enough at dinner ... and then feel hungry later.

Miss the bus and pay me to take him to school.

Etc.

Larry had a mom with a totally different attitude. Instead of fearing mistakes, she was looking forward to them. One morning, she saw him heading out the door without his lunchbox. Pinching her lips together with all ten fingers, she resisted the urge to remind him. Whispering to herself, she repeated, "Affordable mistake ... affordable mistake ... affordable mistake ..."

Mom was surprised to get no phone call from school that day. She was also surprised that Larry didn't say anything about it when he got home. She was *not* surprised when Larry inhaled two helpings at dinner. The only thing that came out of her mouth was something like, "I noticed that you forgot your lunch. That must have been upsetting."

Way to go, Mom!

The next morning was the true test of Mom's resolve. As Larry walked out the door without his lunch, all ten of her fingers barely mustered the strength to plaster her mouth shut. "Affordable mistake ... affordable mistake ... affordable mistake ..." kept ringing in her head. Thirty seconds later, the door burst open, Larry ran in, he grabbed his lunch, and he proclaimed, "Oh man! I almost forgot!"

The bus rolled away that morning with a much wiser boy.

© 2002 Charles Fay, Ph.D.

Understanding Kids Who Hate School
By Foster W. Cline, M.D.

VOL. 18, NO. 1

When children hate school and don't do well in one class or another, it can be a complicated diagnostic problem. It may require professional expertise to sort out.

However, it may be a lot easier to sort out than one might imagine. It's not always all that complicated. And it's very important to sort out school and learning problems. For if the school and parents see the problem as a learning problem, when the real problem is resistance, the child may become more resistant. On the other hand, parents and schools may believe there is a primary attitude or resistance problem when really, the foundation problem is actually a learning difference.

Finally, within the problems that appear as a learning disturbance, many of those difficulties may be a simple motor output delay that is *really no problem at all* in the long run. I have found that parents and even some teachers lose all sight of common sense around academic underperformance. The feelings and attitudes of the children somehow get lost. Getting that homework *done*, and obtaining high grades, supersede the recognition and appreciation of good relationships, responsible behavior, and high achievement in other nonacademic areas. And study after study shows it is these latter accomplishments that bear most strongly on adult high achievement.

To best get a line on your child's poor school achievement, answer seven simple questions "yes" or "no." If the answer is not an obvious "yes" or "no," then leave it blank. If you leave most blank, you either don't know your kid, or are just too darn wishy-washy yourself! For a perceptual check, have another adult who knows the child well also answer the seven simple questions.

1. My child is basically cooperative and does his or her chores.
2. My child and I have a good basic relationship.

3. Are you, yourself, generally responsible and high-achieving?
4. Is your child without developmental or neurologic handicaps?
5. Does your child do all right in some classes and not in others?
6. Is there a family history of learning disorders?
7. Does your child have problems getting things down on paper? Are handwriting and pictures more scrubby than for most children his or her age? (For instance, most children can adequately draw circles at three, squares at four, triangles at five, diamonds at six.)

"No" on the First Three Questions

Questions 1, 2, 3 are indicators of general cooperation and responsiveness. If your child has trouble emptying the trash, gives you grief when you ask for a simple job to be done, and/or has a poor relationship with you, you need, first off, to start using Love and Logic parenting principles. The academic problem is secondary. When you get to the point that you can answer "yes" on the first three questions, academic achievement may automatically improve. Good, responsive relationships are important for school achievement. Obviously a child may have poor responsiveness *and* learning problems too—they often go together—but the first thing to concentrate on is not academic achievement but improvement in across-the-board attitude and responsiveness. I've seen a lot of good taxpayer money wasted when a learning problem is diagnosed and the real difficulty is poor behavior and poor general responsiveness or passive resistance. As a general rule, most children won't do their homework much better than they empty the trash!

"Yes" on the First Three Questions

Generally, if your child is loving, responsive, and cooperative at home but has achievement and attitude problems about school, it is not, *at the foundation,* a general cooperation or attitude problem. This doesn't mean that your child has a good attitude about school but simply that attitude may not the *crux* of the issue. What's more, if your child continues to have a good relationship with you, and you, yourself, are cooperative and high-achieving, the most effective thing you can do is stand back and let your child unfold before your dumfounded eyes.

Great little kids who have problems in school and no obvious neurologic problems (Question 4) are often simply late bloomers. School is harder for them than for other kids, and then they develop secondary attitude problems. It is not the attitude that causes the problems, it is problems that cause an attitude issue.

There are late bloomers! It is a politically incorrect thing to say in this day of "mandatory diagnosis and remediation for every academically underachieving kid," but the truth is, if the parent–child relationship remains good, all will probably turn out fine in the long run.

Remember, half the kids are in the lower half of the developmental curve, and one out of four boys is in the lower fourth of the male developmental curve. And while you may say, "Well, duh!" the average reader would be shocked at how often folks forget that one-fourth of kids developmentally have three-fourths of the kids ahead of them and that this is *perfectly normal, A-okay, and generally no cause for concern!* Especially if your child wishes he was doing better.

There is a great truth: *If you have a great little kid who doesn't do that well in school and wishes he did better, you are generally home free!*

So, if you answered "yes" on the first three questions and your child has problems in school achievement, then the *most common* answers are:

1. There is a developmental delay, and when they are older, they will take off when they are able and something that excites them comes along. Relax.
2. There are peer problems. Often kids who turn out to be real winners as adults don't get along well with kids their own age. They don't relate to all of that childhood nonsense from other kids. They simply have a different maturity level. They hate school because of conflicted relationships.

3. There are problems with a particular subject and/or a particular teacher. Adults focus on excitement about the subject, and to heck if we like the professor. For kids it's the opposite. *Children focus on their love (or lack of it) for the teacher and to heck with the subject.* When children love the teacher, they tend do well. When adults love the subject, they do well.

"Yes" on Question 4

The problem is usually obvious and good professional help goes a long way. Give your child the "can do" message. Keep your expectations reasonably high. Walk that thin line between making allowances for the problem without allowing the problem to be an excuse. It's tough. But remember, your child should do as well for you as he or she does at summer camp for strangers. It is easy to confuse the "won'ts" and the "can'ts" with obviously challenged children. And when children have a neurologic or obvious developmental problem, *it is still the good relationship with the parents that carries the day.* So with most developmentally disturbed children, it is better always to concentrate on the relationships than on the academics. Both are important. But keep your priorities straight. When parents get so upset about how their child is doing in school that they lose the good relationship, they are being self-defeating. I've seen that happen over and over again.

"Yes" on Question 5

Your child is having problems with the kids, the discipline, the teacher, or the subject matter in a particular class. Attempt to sort that out. The only way to know is by *listening* to—not talking to—your child. Listening is always better than a lecture!

If the problem is the teacher, the subject, or the other kids, Love and Logic encourages parents to be slow to rescue, for every rescue covertly gives a child the "You can't cope" message. It's often better to take the tack, "Yeah, that is a really tough teacher, but if anyone can learn to handle someone like that, it's you!" If *everyone* knows it is a hopeless situation, and your child knows that he can't cope, and you know he can't cope, and he knows that you know he can't cope, then pull him out of the class. It's a sad situation but sometimes necessary.

"Yes" on Question 6

Lots of specific learning problems are inherited. Although remediation may help, if the problem is in math, for instance, your child should plan on growing up and having an accountant help with the tax forms. I, myself, fall into this category. Sometimes it's just better to give up and buy a compass than have a class in "directional remediation." I once saw one poor eighth-grader who had an inherited problem with numbers—a young woman who hated school. She was in two remedial math classes and her parents (good luck with that, kid!) were attempting to help her with math homework. I did a little research and found that one really only needs to know sixth-grade math to do okay in life. She knew sixth-grade math. So I "treated" her by taking her out of all math classes and substituting classes she would like. What a turnaround! She was a different person! Let's not continually butt our heads against the wall trying to pound things into kids that they may never get or will naturally get later! Remember, there are lots of infants who don't walk until fourteen months, and do just fine without a walking remediation class.

"Yes" on Question 7

Many times, a simple motor output problem is mistaken for a learning problem. Many little boys really do "get it"; they just can't prove it because their handwriting is so slow and sloppy. Much of the time this common problem is outgrown. Far too many kids are considered "smart" because they get things down on paper neat and fast, or "dumb" because they are slow and messy.

I feel real sad for kids who are in the class of a "neatness freak" teacher who concentrates on how their papers look when, in reality, whether the teacher makes their life miserable by requesting papers to be done over and over or relaxes a bit, the child will be doing fine by young adulthood if their self-image is kept high.

There is an old saying, "One-third of third-grade boys reverse letters one-third of the time." And while this is not true in many schools, the point is that most kids of normal intelligence who letter-reverse won't be reversing letters as adults. If the answers to the first three questions were "yes," then relax and keep your child's self-image high, and all will work out okay in the long run.

Depressed Teens Don't Have to Feel So Bad!
By Charles Fay, Ph.D.
VOL. 18, NO. 2

Let's hear the good news first! There's no need for a teenager ... or anyone else ... to spend their time feeling sad, worthless, and hopeless.

There are many very successful treatments for depression.

About 20 percent of teens are caught in the grips of this potentially life-threatening illness. Unfortunately, many suffer without benefiting from effective treatment. Some quietly withdraw. Others act out their pain, get in trouble with authority, and are misdiagnosed as either "behavior disordered" or simply a "pain in the butt." Sadly, some decide that life isn't worth living.

I received a letter not long ago from a very worried mother. It read something like the following:

We don't know what to do with our fifteen-year-old daughter. We can't believe that such a wonderful kid feels so bad about herself.

She hardly leaves her room. When she does, she's so irritable that it's hard not to snap back at her. Something negative always comes out of her mouth. She accuses us of being "mean," "unfair," or not understanding how she feels. In the next breath, she tells us how "worthless" or "stupid" she is.

Yesterday, she left school during lunch, walked to a friend's house near the school, and drank so much Vodka that she could barely walk. When she staggered back into school, she was expelled on the spot.

Love and Logic doesn't seem to be working. She doesn't care about consequences or anything else. What do we do?

Depression is most often the result of three overlapping causes:

• Chemical imbalances in parts of the brain that regulate emotions
• Stress resulting from family, peer, school, or other problems
• Negative thinking habits

Listed below are tips for helping a depressed teen. Most important, take decisive action. Don't ignore the problem. Serious depression won't cure itself.

Don't fall into the trap of assuming that all teenagers are sullen and irritable.

Believe it or not, most teenagers are pretty fun to be around! Although adolescence is a time of challenges and changes, most kids get through it *without* being chronically withdrawn, sullen, and angry.

I cringe every time I hear an educator or parent say something like, "What do you expect? He's a teenager."

Sadly, this attitude stands in the way of many teens receiving the treatment they need. If any of the following symptoms continue for more than two weeks, contact a qualified mental health professional:

• Feeling of sadness, guilt, worthlessness, or hopelessness
• Angry outbursts
• Withdrawal from friends and family
• Lack of interest or enthusiasm in typically fun activities
• Irritability and argumentativeness

- Restlessness and agitation
- Poor performance in school
- Defiance toward parents, teachers, and other authority figures
- Changes in eating and sleeping patterns (either an increase or decrease)
- Problems with concentration and memory
- Substance abuse and other risky behaviors

Be aware that teenage depression has many faces.
Did you know that some depressed adolescents try to cope with their pain by acting out? As you noticed above, some use one or more of the following disruptive, risky behaviors as a way of avoiding the hurt in their hearts:

- Reckless driving
- Cigarette smoking, alcohol, or drugs
- Sexual promiscuity
- Shoplifting or other illegal activities

Increase supervision and remove dangerous items from the home.
According to the National Mental Health Association, suicide is the third leading cause of death in adolescents.

Wise parents of depressed kids don't take chances. Believing it's "better to be safe than sorry," they do their very best to make sure that their children spend as little time as possible unsupervised.

Wise parents also remove or lock up the following items:

- Guns, knives, and other weapons
- Prescription and nonprescription medications
- Car keys

An automobile can be a very powerful instrument of self-destruction. Seriously depressed teens should not be allowed use of the family car.

Consult with a qualified child and adolescent psychiatrist.
There is no substitute for qualified professional help. Most experts agree: most instances of depression have a strong physical or biological basis. Therefore, medication is often an essential part of effective treatment.

Child and adolescent psychiatrists specialize in this area of treatment and are the only professionals qualified to prescribe medications for kids suffering from mental illness.

Encourage your teen to participate in therapy.
The most successful treatment involves a combination of medication *and* therapy.

Place responsibility for happiness on your teen's shoulders.
Some parents make the mistake of becoming overly emotional and overly involved in their teen's depression. When their kid gets upset, they get upset. When their child mopes around the house, these parents spend all of their energy trying to be therapists or cheerleaders. Some even make the mistake of thinking that buying "stuff" for their youngster will solve the problem. Through their words and actions, these parents unintentionally send this message:

This is horrible and terrible. It's so bad, and you are so incapable that I need to solve this problem for you.

Wiser parents express empathy and listen, while placing full responsibility for happiness on their child's shoulders. Verbally and nonverbally, they communicate:

I know you are hurting. I also know that you are strong enough to take responsibility for your own emotions.

To accomplish this, effective parents are constantly expressing empathy and constantly saying the following things:

"I know you are hurting."

"What are you going to do to feel better?"

"What did your therapist suggest?"

"Would you like my some ideas from me?"

"Whatever you decide, we'll love you."

"Good luck."

Maintain limits and high expectations.

Some parents of depressed kids make the mistake of backing down on limits and lowering expectations for respectful behavior. These parents care deeply for their youngsters yet live by the mistaken belief that their children shouldn't be expected to be responsible or respectful because they are hurting inside. Ironically, their kids get even more depressed, sullen, and irresponsible. Without limits, kids feel lost and unloved. When they act out or display disrespectful behavior, they are really *screaming,* "Please love me enough to set some limits!"

When parents maintain firm yet loving discipline, they help their depressed kids feel safe and hopeful. They also teach their kids an essential life lesson ... how to muster the strength to keep going, even when the going gets really tough.

Communicate unconditional love.

Unconditional love does not mean that we agree with or condone everything our kids believe or do. Rather, it simply means that we will love them regardless of what they achieve, how they look, what they believe, etc. This message is *extremely* healing!

During my training as a school psychologist, I worked almost exclusively with very aggressive, violent kids. As a result, I was starting to get a bit depressed! Because I was seeing so little progress with these extremely disturbed kids, my supervisor suggested that I take on a different type of case ... a very nice fifteen-year-old girl who spent most of each school day crying in the nurse's office.

I remember my first meeting with Sara. Tears streamed down her cheeks, her hair looked like a rat's nest, and all she could say was, "I hate myself."

Following the guidelines suggested above, her parents and teachers saw dramatic changes in less than four months. A year later, I had the wonderful opportunity to visit with Sara. In front of me sat a completely different kid ... hope had replaced her hopelessness, and a smile had replaced her tears.

There is great hope!

The following websites provide additional helpful information:

www.nmha.org (National Institute of Mental Health)
www.drada.org (Depression and Related Affective Disorders Association)

When Is Stepping In, Helping Out, and Rescuing Warranted?
By Foster W. Cline, M.D.

VOL. 18, No. 2

I have heard parents say, "I'm a Love and Logic parent, so I didn't rescue him from the situation." Sometimes it is almost said with a bit of pride, "I let my child learn." Sometimes that is understandable, because parents who used to rescue their child can feel such *freedom* when they realize that they increase their child's ability to cope by letting their children wrestle with consequences. Recently I was involved in a dispute in which a number of parents were offended because of the language a coach used in front of the children. The coach was well liked by the kids, and they told their parents "Don't worry about it." However, one parent proclaimed, "It bothers me, and deep down I'm sure it must bother Janette." I remember thinking, "Wow, what a quandary, you've raised a daughter who can cope and handle things better than you, and it must be hard to accept."

Love and Logic teaches that rescue almost always makes people weaker. However, Love and Logic has two great thoughts on rescuing:

1. The more you rescue your child, the more you will guarantee their failure.
2. No matter what the problem, if the creator demands or expects rescue, the rescue will not result in a change in behavior.

There are many situations in which rescue is warranted:

1. It is warranted when life or long-term health is at probable or definite risk. (Too often we rush in to "save a child" when in fact life or health are not at risk.)
2. Rescue is warranted when our responsible children make a request to be helped out in a situation that is not recurrent. For example, a child who is responsible forgets to take something to school, and asks politely, *without the demand,* that a parent bring it to the school. If you would do it for a friend, do it for your kid! I can't tell you how many times my wife has helped me out when I have forgotten something. Because that is not my "lifestyle," and not chronic, she is "safe" in helping out.
3. Many of our special needs children require more than the average structure, and sometimes require rescue from situations that they may have played a part in bringing on. This is the case when children lack good causal thinking, and no matter how much they suffer, they have problems making wise decisions and planning ahead. If allowing a person to suffer brings no long-term good results, then simply standing by while the suffering occurs over and over again is hard on our soul.
4. We should rescue our children from a situation in which we know they are unable to cope. Especially if they know we are aware that they are unable to cope. Rescue of children really says, "You can't cope with this by yourself." If that *is* the case and everyone knows it, and it's *not* going to change, then rescue your kid.

5. Rescue or help in a situation may be warranted when we are doing it for the good of the child's environment.

Let me give an example. When my daughter was eleven, she had a disturbed sixth-grade teacher we will call Mr. Smith. My wife and I handled it with Love and Logic: "Lucky for you that you are learning now, at age eleven, how to handle people who are unjust and treat you unfairly." We emphasized how all great leaders learn to handle tough situations. This is what sets us above the masses who have trouble coping in rough times. We affirmed that anyone can handle a great teacher, but real leadership develops when we learn how to handle a very difficult one. We celebrated her coming up with internal and external ploys to minimize the effect of her teacher's certifiably crazy behavior. Our daughter, with our encouragement, coped well with a very difficult situation, and came through it with flying colors. In fact, when in a tough situation, as an adult, she laughs, copes, and handles it by saying, "It's just a 'Smith situation.' No problem."

However, on giving a talk in the town she grew up in, I was reminded by a woman our daughter's age how many students had been injured by that teacher when parents handled it in a more hand-wringing and protective way. She said, "I wish my parents had handled it like you did, but they didn't, and I still have nightmares about him. I think most parents, like mine, handled it with anxiety and upset in front of their kids and by doing so he hurt a lot of us."

Now, older and wiser, I think sometimes we might step into a situation to rescue children when it could actually be used as a great challenge and a learning experience for our child's coping and leadership skills.

© 2002 Foster W. Cline, M.D.

How to Raise a Trophy Kid
By Jim Fay

VOL. 18, NO. 3

Marge was at it again: "Coach Templeton had no business singling out Josh like that. Josh isn't the first kid to break team rules. It happens all the time. Besides, those rules are unreasonable in the first place. All teenagers drink. That's part of growing up. What you people are doing is robbing him of his future athletic scholarship. There goes his professional career. And it's all because of your silly rules. I'm calling our lawyer and we'll see how long you keep your precious job!"

This isn't the first time Marge has stood between Josh's bad decisions and the consequences of his actions. She has a history of trying to make Josh look good regardless of his behavior. As a result, her precious boy's success has become increasingly dependent upon his parents, and less related to his effort and responsibility.

In reviewing Josh's school records we find that Marge blamed the elementary school teachers for his poor grades. She demanded that he be given better grades because the teachers were unfair. In fifth grade his inappropriate fondling of a girl on the school bus was excused because Marge threw a fit over the lack of adequate bus supervision and threatened to take her case to the superintendent.

During Josh's middle school years, Marge was frequently seen at school making sure that he had the "right" teachers and that any grade less than an A was adjusted. Josh was frequently given extra-credit work so that he could raise his grades. Teachers often complained to the administration about his preferential treatment and eventually discovered that his parents were doing much of his homework and projects for him.

When confronted with these concerns, Marge maintained, "You don't understand. I love my son. He has to know that I'm here for him. I have an obligation to make sure he feels good about himself so he can develop a good self-concept."

Josh is now in his senior year of high school. He has all the latest electronic gadgets, the best clothes his parents can afford, his own car, and appears to the outside world as if he has the world on a string. As you can guess, he has earned none of these trappings of success. Unfortunately, we see many teens growing up the same way. And as a professional who has worked with families for almost fifty years, I see more and more kids like Josh every year.

Let's stop right here and ask this question: "Am I talking about a majority of teenagers and their parents?" No, but are you also seeing an increasing number of parents like Marge? These are parents who are making extraordinary efforts and sacrifices to be sure that their kids look good to the outside world. Who goes out of their way to create a perfect life for their kids?

My experience is that kids who grow up like Josh are shocked, and often demoralized, when they discover that they can't maintain the perfect life that was created for them.

If truth be known, Josh is not really a part of the family. He lives in the home as an "honored guest." He makes few, if any, contributions to the family. He doesn't do his fair share of the work. His parents excuse this away by saying that his real job is to get a good education so that he can be successful after leaving home.

What a joke this is. We already know that Josh is putting in minimal effort in this area. Is it possible that his poor misguided parents truly believe that good grades, many of which are the result of their intimidation of teachers, actually mean that he has a good education? Could they possibly believe that he is ready for the real world even though he has not had to struggle to earn what he has?

The car, the phone, the clothes, the gadgetry, and even his school grades come more from his parents' efforts than from his own. Sadly, his parents look on with pride at their trophy kid as if he is one more indicator for the outside world that they are successful. Josh serves as an icon of their success much like their luxury car, their home, and their other trappings of success.

Now that the school wants to hold Josh accountable for his rule violations, Marge is faced with the possibility of her trophy becoming tarnished. What will others think if she allows the school and its arbitrary rules to interfere with his perfect image? It appears that Marge's instinctive drive to protect her young has misfired and is running out of control. She is once more ready to do battle with anyone who will interfere with Josh's bump-free ride through life.

All healthy adults are endowed with an instinctual drive to protect children from physical harm. If it were not for this, the human species would not have survived. Unfortunately, many parents were led to believe that this means that we are to protect kids from being uncomfortable. There is a vast difference between protecting kids from life-threatening episodes and protecting them from discomfort.

People who grow up with the realization that misbehavior causes discomfort and inconvenience develop the strength and resilience required to succeed as adults. They also gain character and responsibility that comes from an inner voice that says, "I wonder how my next decision is going to affect me and others?"

Nature provides a great example of this. When we examine the rings of a tree, we discover that some of the rings are wide while others are very narrow. Experts tell us that the wide rings represent a year of growth when life was easy and the tree was able to grow fast. A narrow ring represents a difficult year when the tree was forced to struggle against the elements. Little growth took place that year.

Tree experts will also tell us that the strength of the tree can be measured by the narrow rings. These rings are strong while the wide rings are weak. A tree without a lot of narrow rings is not strong enough to stand by itself for very long.

Our kids are no different. Kids who are protected from their struggles become weak. They don't develop beliefs that success and achievement come from their own effort. When faced with disappointments or challenges they look to others instead of themselves for comfort and success.

Getting back to Marge and Josh's problem, Marge had two choices. She could either stand between his bad decisions and the consequence, or she could stand beside him as he learned from them. Unfortunately, she believes that a mother's job is to choose the former. In reality she has decided to steal Josh's opportunity to become strong on his own. This meets her own needs to feel like a good mother and negates Josh's needs to learn to stand on his own two feet.

I hope you are not raising a trophy kid. The trouble with trophies is that they usually end up sitting around gathering dust and many end up in the thrift store.

© 2002 Jim Fay

When's It Time for Kids to Make Their Own Choices?
By Foster W. Cline, M.D.
VOL. 18, NO. 3

Love and Logic parents often ask, "When do I allow my kids to make some choices that I don't feel that great about?"

During the very early years, giving choices is pretty easy, and the choices we give are simplistic:

"Would you like to put your left foot in first, or your right?"
"Would you like to wear your blue dress or the yellow one?"

Allowing children to make small choices builds a "bank account" of control that parents can use when the going gets tough. If we give enough little choices when things are going well, we can make some "withdrawals" from this account when they aren't:

"You got to decide what cereal you wanted, what bowl you
    wanted, the type of juice you wanted to drink. Now it's my
    turn for a choice and my choice is that we leave at 8:00 sharp."

Now let's get something straight. Love and Logic parents don't give their kids choices over everything! Sometimes it's our job to boss our kids around a bit.

Love and Logic parents never hesitate to boss their kids around when choices might cause life-or-death consequences!

Love and Logic parents *do not say*, "Honey, would you like to run out into traffic or would you rather hold my hand?" Love and Logic parents give reasonable choices because there are many benefits:

- Choices simply cut down on the number of power struggles we see.
- Choices also help kids develop a healthy understanding of cause and effect. When we allow our kids to make small mistakes over small issues, they learn how to avoid life-or-death mistakes over life-or-death issues. I'd much rather a child be unhappy with the cereal they choose at *nine* years old than the spouse they choose at *twenty-nine*.
- Finally, a child's ability to make wise choices, followed by the parent's show of pleasure in those choices, definitely builds feelings of competency and self-esteem.

But let's get back to our question. When should kids be allowed to make some choices we don't necessarily like? When children are small they can almost always be led into choices that we both *approve of* and *accept*.

As children approach adolescence, and begin to think much more abstractly and independently, they will try out many ideas and make many choices that parents don't necessarily like.

Strange as it may sound, when children make decisions that parents aren't joyful about, they're actually preparing themselves for leadership. Leadership involves making decisions that many people don't like but must accept. Through inspiration and results, a true and talented leader eventually brings most people to respect and approve of the decision. We only step in when the consequences are life-or-death or would create a major problem for us.

There are some wonderful things that can happen when our kids make decisions that don't meet our approval. If the decision turns out to be a poor one:

1. There are almost always natural consequences. Our children can learn and cope with these consequences when we remain empathetic and avoid the temptation to rescue.
2. Our youngsters are forced to reason, "My wise parents were right again." Each time this happens, they respect us more.

If the decision we don't like turns out to be right, there can be benefits as well. History is filled with extremely successful people who've made wise decisions that seemed unwise to their parents:

1. Children learn that authority figures don't always have all the answers, and independent thinking on their own may be called for. (This will serve her well when as president she has to make tough calls when her expert advisers are all wrong.)
2. Children learn that taking some *thoughtful* risks is a part of living a fulfilling life.

When our kids are young, we can almost always talk them into making the choices we like—as their hormones and minds grow, we cannot keep them from making some choices that we don't necessarily like. Fortunately, everyone can be a winner. If we maintain a loving relationship, remain empathetic, and avoid rescuing, our kids can win ... and so can we!

The Evolution of the Helicopter Parent: The Turbo-Attack Helicopter Model
By Jim Fay
VOL. 18, No. 4

A joke hit the Internet recently. The problem is that it is not a joke. It's a serious concern to all those who work with today's youth. A high school staff met to design the perfect recording for their telephone answering machine. The staff looked at several possibilities and finally agreed on the following:

To lie about why your child is absent – Press 1

*To make excuses for why your child did not do his work
    – Press 2*

To complain about what we do – Press 3

To swear at staff members – Press 4

*To ask why you didn't get information that was already enclosed
    in your newsletter and several flyers mailed to you – Press 5*

If you want us to raise your child – Press 6

*If you want to reach out and touch, slap, or hit someone
    – Press 7*

To request another teacher for the third time this year – Press 8

To complain about bus transportation – Press 9

To demand that your child get a higher grade – Press 0

*If you realize this is the real world and your child must be
    accountable/responsible for his/her own behavior, classwork,
    and homework, and that it's not the teacher's fault for your
    child's lack of effort, hang up and have a great day.*

I have consulted in many schools and know how overloaded teachers are today. I have witnessed the fact that teachers don't have enough spare time during the day to eat or go to the bathroom, let alone to do all the things society asks of them. This being true, why do you suppose a staff would spend its time fantasizing about this kind of thing?

Sad to say, the teachers are recognizing a national epidemic. It's the "Jet-Powered Turbo-Attack Helicopter Model" epidemic. It rears its ugly head in all communities, but is especially excessive and out of control in the more affluent communities, where parents have the financial resources and power to intimidate schools and community agencies.

If this is not you, just read on for the enjoyment.

Many of today's parents are obsessed with the desire to create a perfect image for their kids. This perfect image, or perfect life, is one in which their kids never have to face struggle, inconvenience, discomfort, or disappointment. It is a life in which the child can be launched into adulthood with the best of credentials. These kids look great on paper. Their high school and college diplomas show high grades even if they were not earned. They lead a life where their mistakes are swept under the table. I have often heard these parents say, "It's a competitive world out there and I want my kids to have every advantage. What they do when they are young should not hold them back later."

These parents, in their zeal to protect their young, swoop down like jet-powered, attack helicopters on any person or agency who might hold their children accountable for their actions. Armed with verbal smart bombs, they are quick to blast away at anyone who sets high standards for behavior, morality, or achievement.

Declaring their child a victim is a favorite tactical maneuver designed to send school personnel diving into the trenches for protection. Teachers and school administrators become worn down by this constant barrage. As they give in to parental demands that their children not be held accountable, standards are eroded and teachers gradually think, "What's the use?"

It is horribly disappointing to watch kids learn to blame others for their lack of success instead of becoming people who reach goals through effort and determination.

All this has caused me to look back thirty years to the time when we first wrote about Helicopter parents. I now realize that those parents were relatively harmless compared to the modern-day version. I daily hear about the "turbo jet-powered models" designed for deadly attack. Some of these parents are not satisfied with protection, but even prefer to destroy the infrastructure of the very agencies that are dedicated to helping their children grow into educated, moral human beings.

Now you tell me. Is it possible for children who have never had to stand on their own two feet, never had to be responsible for their own actions, or never had to face and solve the smaller problems of childhood, to have the tools to face the rigors of adult life in America? We all know the answer to that.

Can the young adult who gets that perfect job perform well enough to keep that job if his grades from school were the result of teacher intimidation instead of vigorous study? The company who hires this person won't be easily intimidated by parental pressure in the face of substandard performance.

A perfect image and perfect school transcript are poor substitutes for character and the attitude that achievement comes through struggle and perseverance.

I have worked with many parents who have fallen into this trap. They all love their children. They all want the best for them. They talk about how they don't want their kids to struggle like they did. They are prone to rush to blame others for any lack of achievement on their children's part. These parents are willing to hold others responsible for their children's actions.

However, they are often willing to change their parenting style once they see its crippling effects. Many of these parents have said to me, "I now realize that even if I succeed in creating a perfect life for my kid, there is little chance that they can maintain it without my help."

Your Child Can Rise to the Top
One very astute father once said to me, "Jim, I've got it. There is a huge group of trophy kids growing up today who won't have the character and resilience to compete in the labor market. If my kid grows up knowing how to get what he wants through struggle and character, he will be the one with the true advantage. He will stand head and shoulders above the others because he has the tools to create his own perfect life. Now that I have learned that I can discipline my child without losing his love, I have the courage to abandon my old, crippling parenting style. The Love and Logic approach to raising my kid will give all of us the tools it takes to make this happen."

© 2003 Jim Fay

When Parents Have Different Parenting Styles: Believe It or Not ... Kids Can Handle It!

By Charles Fay, Ph.D.

Vol. 18, No. 4

My husband (or wife) isn't interested in using Love and Logic. He (or she) handles the kids much differently than I do. What do I do?

My ex-husband (or ex-wife) rescues the kids (or bosses them around). How do I get him (or her) to stop?

In our travels across the country, these questions are some of the most common we hear. Why? Because people often fall in love with those who "fill" a part of them they see as missing. Introverted Ivan falls in love with Outgoing Alice. Sloppy Stan marries Neat Nancy. Careful Curtis finds Wild Wendy irresistible. Passive Patty is drawn like a magnet to Take-Charge Tom.

The very qualities that pull us together often become those that threaten to push us apart. What an irony! Fortunately, kids don't need carbon-copy parents ... as long as their parents agree to live by some basic guidelines:

Agree to make each other look good in the eyes of your children.
Don't put your kids in the "best friend" or "counselor" roles! Too often, parents complain to their kids about the other parent: "Your father (or mother) just doesn't understand. If he (or she) would just listen ..."

This places kids in a terrible bind. Should kids be solving their parent's problems? Absolutely not!

This also makes one parent into the "bad guy." Soon, children learn how to take advantage of this situation for manipulative ends. How sad for everyone.

When we're upset with our spouse, we must resist the incredibly attractive urge to agree with our kids when they say things like, "Dad doesn't understand" or "Mom's mean!" When we're upset with our spouse ... or ex-spouse ... we must discuss it directly with our spouse ... or ex-spouse. Let's keep our kids out of the middle.

Agree that consistency and follow-through are more important than "perfect parenting."

Because they disagree about discipline, some parents make the mistake of undermining the limits and consequences set by the other. This always backfires, creating kids who disrespect *both* parents. Deep in their subconscious minds, children begin to reason, "If my parents aren't strong enough to support each other, how will they ever be strong enough to keep me safe and show me the way?"

Let's take a look at just one potential parental disagreement:

Travis accidentally threw his baseball through a window in the home. As a consequence, Dad has grounded him for two weeks. Travis's mother disagrees with her husband's approach. She thinks it would be better if Travis wasn't grounded but had to pay for the window out of his allowance.

Is it wiser for Mom to "correct" Dad's approach? Or would it be smarter for her to support Dad over this issue and talk with him privately about it later? While Mom may not agree with Dad's stance, it will clearly do more harm for her to undermine him than for Travis to be grounded for two weeks. If Dad is undermined, how open will he be to considering Mom's ideas later? Not very! If she supports him in the short term, is there a better chance he will change his tune in the future? You bet!

Here's the question we must ask ourselves:

Is my spouse (or ex-spouse) behaving in an abusive fashion?

If the answer to this question is no, but we'd like him/her to consider acting differently in the future, we'd better back him/her up and discuss this later by saying:

Honey, remember when you grounded Travis for breaking the window? I didn't want to undermine you in front of him, so I kept my mouth shut. Would you be willing to consider experimenting with something a bit different next time?

Agree to be different.

Our world is filled with different types of people. Some are easy-going. Some are not. Some are very warm. Others are a bit cooler. Some have very high expectations. Some don't. Do we do our kids any favors when we try to shield them from this reality as they are growing up?

When parents agree that it's okay to be different, and they don't fall into the trap of undermining or complaining about each other, their children have a powerful opportunity to learn how to get along with different types of people. Have you ever met an adult who never learned this?

Two friends of mine have a very effective way of answering their children when they hear things like, "Well, Mom says that I can ..." or "Dad's mean." It goes something like the following:

CHILD: "Dad lets me watch TV after 7:30."

MOM: (with excitement and a big smile) "Wow! You are so lucky to have a dad who lets you do that. That is great! Some kids have parents who do everything the same. How boring that would be."

CHILD: "So can I watch this show tonight?"

MOM: (very sweetly) "This is sad. No. Thanks for understanding."

Remember that lectures work no better with spouses than they do with kids.

People often ask, "How do I get my spouse to use Love and Logic?" Listed below are some tactics to *avoid:*

• Saying something like this to your spouse: "You have so much potential as a parent. But you just aren't applying yourself."

- Putting your spouse on a point system where he/she can earn extra privileges based on the conscientious application of Love and Logic principles.
- Gushing with enthusiasm each evening as you give your spouse a three-hour overview of Love and Logic, how wonderful it is, and how it will save them from parenting purgatory.

All joking aside, it's best to take a low-key approach and to remember that modeling is the most powerful tool for creating change in resistant kids ... and adults. Let your spouse see you having more fun and fewer power struggles with the kids. Share some Love and Logic only if they ask about it.

If you can't agree to make each other look good, go to couples counseling. When parents sabotage each other, their children always suffer. It's also not uncommon for kids to be blamed for the problem. Too frequently, I hear people complain, "The kids are driving us nuts. If they weren't so difficult, our marriage would be okay."

While difficult kids can really stress a marriage, the following statement often rings truer: "If our marriage wasn't driving us nuts, the kids wouldn't be so difficult."

It's almost impossible to be a healthy parent when one's marriage is unhealthy. If this is the case, give yourself ... and your kids ... a gift by seeking couples counseling.

There's good news!
Parents don't have to be clones of each other to raise great kids. Thank goodness! My father (yes, that's Jim Fay!) often remarks about how very different his own parents were. His father parented with lectures, threats, and plenty of decibels. His mother was pretty much a Love and Logic natural. What made it possible for them to raise such a fine man? Simply put, my Grandma Marie did her best to make grandpa look good. And to the best of his ability, Grandpa Frank did the same for her.

© 2003 Charles Fay, Ph.D.

Follies of Youth—Our Own and Our Kids'

By Foster W. Cline, M.D.

VOL. 18, NO. 4

Paul looked at me with worried eyes following a workshop. A good father, he was concerned about his son. On most issues, Paul was not at a loss for words. But this was a tough issue. He was concerned that his son Jeff could be experimenting with drugs. And because Paul himself had experimented with drugs in his own adolescence, he didn't know what to say. He didn't even know how to approach the subject.

It was his hot button, and as is often the case in such situations, it is easy to react with impotent frustration.

The following five steps are guidelines on how to deal with such "hot button" issues:

1. Plan what you are going to say. Practice it.
2. Choose the right time for discussion. Don't try to talk to your teens or preteens while they are getting ready for school or an activity.
3. Many parents find that a good time to talk is during a drive. They are with their child in a relatively intimate and uninterrupted space. Too much attention needs to be paid to driving to be frowning at, fighting with, or getting into any knockdown, drag-out discussion. Better yet, everyone knows the time constraints, and that it is best to get to the point and reach a conclusion.
4. Generally, in a "my own youthful folly" issue, it is best to begin by honestly reminiscing about yourself. Generally, if this is done with great thoughtfulness, followed by gentile questions and musings, it will usually lead your children into thoughtful speculations on the way they are handling the same issue in their own lives.
5. Always end by thanking your children for taking time to talk, and let them know how much this means to you.

After talking with Paul, he reported his results to me. This is the way I remember the conversation as he related it to me:

God bless automobile kid deliveries. That is the time to talk! I started by saying that as I looked back on my life, I realized how lucky I was to be alive and have a family. That woke up Jeff, I can tell you!

I told him that I had been looking back on my life and that my teen years seemed fun at the time, but I now realize that they were foolish. I told him that some of my drug-abusing friends were a lot less lucky than I was because their brains didn't work at 100 percent efficiency and that as adults they had trouble keeping a job, or they had problems in relationships probably because of how they had injured their cortexes.

I wondered then if everyone has to learn these things by hard knocks and only in retrospect, or if people do actually learn from the mistakes others tell them about. I wondered if things that adults say to kids really make much difference or if kids need to learn things by themselves, granted that a few might not live through it. Compared to my earlier talks, I came through a lot less judgmental, and lot more speculative and interested.

Jeff opened up. He said most kids had to learn by hard knocks. But he didn't have to. He asked me all about my high school years, the friends I had, the mistakes that I had made. I think it was one of our best conversations. I don't know if he will experiment with drugs or not. It is ultimately his decision, and I let him know it. Love and Logic is clear that there is no sense in trying to control what you obviously can't.

And he knows I won't enable support or rescue. Getting lawyers, going to court with our kids, and raising bail is not part of our family tradition, and he knows I'll carry the "tradition" on with him. We covered all that "Love and Logic, consequences and no rescue" information. But he already knew that.

Although the future is somewhat uncertain, I'm a lot more relaxed knowing that I don't control how things turn out. I only control me. And I know for certain that I was as effec-

tive as I could be. I know we are closer. I know he knows how I feel. And I know that what I think is important to him. So I guess when you are dealing with a teen, that's about the most a parent can hope for.

Paul was happy, and it sounded like he was effective. That was two years ago, and I haven't heard any more concerns about Jeff. So I guess it all worked out.

And it can work for you, too.

© 2003 Foster W. Cline, M.D.

VOLUME
19

A Happy Person vs. a Good Person
By Jim Fay
VOL. 19, NO. 1

CHERYL: "Sam, how could you let me down like this, again? I think you do these things just to undermine what I'm trying to do with our daughter! You know good-and-well why I had to tell her that she couldn't drive for a month. Sara took my car without permission and stayed out all night. I was worried sick! You said you would support me by not letting her drive, and then you turn around and give her your extra car to drive. How are we supposed to make her responsible if you reverse every decision we make?"

SAM: "Now Cheryl, you don't have to be so upset. I was going to call you and tell you that I think you're just overreacting on this. She's just a kid, for Pete's sake! What she's doing is just typical teenage stuff. You need to give her a little slack. Maybe if you'd lighten up a little, you'd both be a lot happier."

CHERYL: "Wait just a minute, Sam! That kind of behavior might be typical for some teenagers, but it's not how all teens act. She's gone way over the line lately! It's getting worse all the time. She doesn't feel that she has any limits at all, and I can see why. Every time she misbehaves, you're there to excuse it away and turn me into the bad guy for trying to hold her accountable for her actions."

Here we see two divorced parents embroiled in a classic struggle. It could be a competition for Sara's love on Sam's part. But it probably goes deeper than that. Sam is a caring man who doesn't like conflict. He lives to make sure that his daughter is always happy. Playing the role of the "good guy" is easy for him. It fits right into his lifelong pattern of conflict avoidance. It also helps him deal with his fear of losing Sara to her mother.

Cheryl, on the other hand, is left with the responsibility of helping their daughter grow into a responsible person. She knows that this can only happen if she sets limits and holds Sara accountable for her actions. But this is difficult for her. It often puts her in the role of the bad guy in her daughter's eyes. Despite this dilemma, she tries to hold the line with Sara even in the face of unintentional but very damaging acts of sabotage by her ex-husband.

Trying to be a good parent, Cheryl is making several mistakes that continue to lock all three into a vicious cycle: Sara misbehaves, Cheryl punishes, and Sam overturns the punishment.

Sam's Mistakes

Sam is willing to sacrifice Sara's long-term happiness and quality of life in exchange for her short-term happiness. He fears the loss of Sara's love and lives with the mistaken idea that she will appreciate and respect him in the role of her protector. Overturning his ex-wife's discipline also gives him a chance to make Mom look bad in his daughter's eyes. He doesn't realize that Sara may eventually view him with contempt for sabotaging her relationship with Mom.

Cheryl's Mistakes

Cheryl holds on to a fantasy that she and Sam are a team. If she couldn't get him to cooperate when they were married, what are the chances that this will happen after they've lived through the pain of divorce? Even though it's unlikely that Sam will suddenly change his tune and begin to back Cheryl's discipline, she holds on to the myth that he will.

Based upon this mistaken idea, Cheryl imposes consequences that must be upheld when her daughter is at Sam's house. This gives Sam both the opportunity and the power to rescind the punishment and place himself in the role of Sara's hero.

Once she gives up the fantasy that her actions will be supported by Sam, she can quit asking him for something he is not able to give. This means Cheryl will start imposing consequences that are carried out only during the time in which Sara is staying at her home. This puts her back in control and reduces some of her disappointment and resulting anger over not being supported.

Cheryl's next mistake is believing that she can make both homes work the same. This is one of the tragedies of divorce. All the energy she uses trying to make this happen is energy that can be spent on things she can actually control.

Her next mistake is trying to reason with Sam about this problem. All her discussions accomplish is to give her ex-husband yet another opportunity to go on the offensive and to attack her parenting attempts. The more she reasons and begs with him, the worse the problem gets.

Cheryl's Solution

Once Cheryl decides to take control of the situation, she will impose consequences that only apply while Sara is with her. If her daughter tries to get Dad to intervene, Cheryl should not allow him to change her mind. She needs to practice the following statement and use it often: "Sam, in the past I have made the mistake of trying to make your home run like my home. I promise not to do that anymore. I won't tell you how to handle Sara when she is with you. If I see her needing discipline when she is with me, I'll handle it here without asking you to deal with it while she's at your place. And you are welcome to do the same."

Her next step is to share her love and her thoughts with Sara. Since their relationship is strained, it is very unlikely that Mom can get all of her thoughts out without facing a counterattack. At times like this, teens are experts at taking parents on "bird walks," arguing each point until both are totally off the subject at hand. What starts out as a discussion soon becomes a fight. Neither person has heard the other.

The solution is for Cheryl to put her thoughts in writing. Notice how her letter begins with a wonderful attention-getting strategy!

Dear Sara,

I need to apologize to you. I'm doing it in writing just in case you want to revisit my thoughts in the future. Please don't feel a need to respond right away. I just want you to think about this for a while.

I have made a big mistake not being open with you about the fact that your dad and I often differ on how to be parents. I have spent too much time trying to make him be the same as I am. That's not fair to you or to him. We both love you very much but have different ways of showing it. By trying to make him do things my way, you have been caught in the middle of our unhappiness. This often happens in marriages and especially happens in divorces.

My way of showing my love for you is to work hard to help you become a good person. To do this, I have to hold you accountable for your actions. This means I also have to be prepared for you to be angry with me in the short term.

The mistake I have been making is to ask your dad to discipline you over things that happen in my house. I'm not going to be doing that anymore. You and I will take care of those problems without involving Dad. Dad can deal with any problems that come up at his house without interference from me. I hope that this will be less confusing for you.

You are growing up with two different kinds of parents. As time goes on, you will have plenty of different thoughts and feelings about both of us. Please remember that we both love you very much. I hope you know that the divorce was not your fault. I hope you know that it's okay to love both Dad and me at the same time.

Love,
Mom

This was a tough letter for Mom to write. There were many things that she wanted to say but knew better. She wanted to share her feelings of anger and hurt toward Sam. She felt a twinge of desire to tell Sara how irresponsible she believes Sam to be. She wanted to scream out, "Your dad is messing up your life! Look at me! I'm the one who *really* cares!"

Instead, Cheryl walked the much healthier and nobler path. Why? Because she realizes that each time she criticizes Dad in her daughter's eyes, she drives her daughter further away. Even though Dad rescues and excuses Sara from her poor decisions, he's an important part of her life. If Mom were to bad-mouth him, it would do much more damage than his rescuing behavior. Sara will learn some positive things from Dad ... and she will learn how to take good care of herself and be responsible from Mom. Mom's staying out of the "blame game" will allow Sara to sit back, watch her parents, and gather what's good from each.

Isn't that what we all want for our kids?

Honesty Deficit Disorder (HDD) ... or, What to Do When Your Kids Lie
By Charles Fay, Ph.D.
VOL. 19, No. 1

How's a parent to respond when their child comes down with the fibber's flu? There are few things that hit the "parental nerve" more soundly than when our kids tell a big fat lie! Responsible parents begin to wonder and worry: "Why did he lie?" "Where did he learn that? We don't live our lives that way!" "What kind of life is he going to have if he keeps this up?"

Wise parents *are* wise to be worried. But wise parents also know that kids are like scientists, constantly experimenting with varying mixtures of misbehavior. To learn about the wonderful world of cause and effect, they must experiment. To help them learn that crime doesn't pay, parents must caringly show them that consequences will follow. Stated differently, it's a kid's job to test limits. It's a parent's job to enforce these limits in a loving way.

But what's a parent to do when their child lies? Let's take a look at what doesn't work:

MOM: "You told me that you were going over to Shawn's to study! I called over there, and his mom said you two went to the mall. You lied to me!"

APRIL:	"We did not! We studied first ... then we just went to hang out for a while."
MOM:	"Let's see your homework. Show me what you did."
APRIL:	"Well ... umm ..."
MOM:	"You lied! Admit it."
APRIL:	"No I didn't! Why are you always on my case? You never trust me!"
MOM:	"Well, if you would just tell the truth, then I'd trust you! That's it! You're grounded!"
APRIL:	"Not fair!"
MOM:	"Yes it is fair! It's about time that ..."

This parent fell into the trap of ranting, raving, and trying to make her child admit to a lie. Why is this a problem? Simply because it drains valuable energy, creates greater parent–child resentment, and shows the child that the best way to get an exciting display of parental frustration and anger is to lie ... and then lie about lying. Did I also mention how this approach takes years off of the parent's life?

Let's take a look at a lower stress, more successful approach. Pay close attention as the parent gives her child the gift of knowing that honesty is the best policy:

WEDNESDAY AFTERNOON

MOM:	"You told me that you were going over to Shawn's to study. I called over there, and his mom said you two went to the mall."
APRIL:	"We did not! We studied first ... then we just went to hang out for a while."
MOM:	"Well, I need to think about this more before I do something. We'll talk later."
APRIL:	"What are you gonna do?"
MOM:	(walking away) "I'm not sure. I need some time to think."

Friday Evening

April: "Mom! We're late! It's time to leave for the rec center! Remember the dance?"

Mom: (with sincere empathy) "This is such a drag. I'll be happy to do the special things I do for you when I can trust that you have been telling the truth."

April: "Not fair!"

Mom: (calmly) "I love you too much to argue."

April: "But it's not fair!"

Mom: (still calmly) "I love you too much to argue ..."

Listed below are a few tips for handling lying without raising your blood pressure.

Instead of responding with anger, lectures, or threats, delay the consequence.

When April caught her off-guard, and Mom was too angry to think straight, she delayed the consequence. This bought her time to visit with friends and to formulate a watertight plan.

Use a strong dose of empathy to show that lying makes your child's life stink.

When Mom responded to April's lie with anger and frustration, she allowed her daughter to reason, "When I lie, it makes my parents really mad. I better not *get caught* next time."

Something very different happened when Mom responded with empathy. Down deep, April was forced to reason, "When I lie, it makes my life really stink. I better make better decisions in the future."

In essence, empathy ups the odds that our kids will make wise decisions even when we aren't around!

Go on strike and negotiate for better working conditions.

April's mom chose a consequence requiring no one else's cooperation than her own. In fact, the only thing we can actually control beyond a shadow of a doubt is our own behavior. This counts double when we're parents of children way too large to carry!

Without lectures, anger, or sarcasm, Mom stopped doing many of the extra things April had become accustomed to. Isn't this similar to what happens in the adult world when one lies to friends, coworkers, etc.?

In just over a week, Mom noticed that April's attitude had become much sweeter. She also noticed that April was willing to do some extra chores to repay the energy she had drained by being dishonest. As April became more responsible, Mom became more willing to drive her where she wanted to go, buy the kind of food she liked, etc.

Trust your parental instincts.
Too many parents doubt themselves when their gut tells them that their kids have lied. Too frequently today's parents feel like they must make their case, beyond a "reasonable doubt," before they feel justified in providing consequences. As a result, their kids are forever leading them on wild goose chases. Soon their children begin to believe that it's okay to lie as long as you can provide a convincing ... or confusing ... counterargument.

Our homes are not courtrooms, and our children should not be treated like defense attorneys or defendants. While Love and Logic parents do their best to listen, be fair, and consider their children's views, they realize that there are times when we must "convict" even when the evidence is merely circumstantial.

When parents apply these practical tips, most kids quickly realize that lying creates more problems for them than it solves. With a sincere serving of Love and Logic, most kids learn that their lives are much happier keeping honesty as their motto.

There are exceptions, however. For various reasons, some children lack good cause-and-effect reasoning when it comes to honesty. Kids who've been abused or neglected sometimes come to believe that lying is the only way they can protect themselves and get their needs met. Children with some types of neurological conditions lack the impulse-control to routinely choose the delayed gratification of being honest over the immediate gratification of lying and getting oneself off the hook ... albeit temporarily. If your child continues to lie on a chronic basis, despite your diligent application of Love and Logic, seek professional help. The sooner you do, the better.

Fortunately, most kids, even those with emotional or behavioral problems, eventually learn that lying to a Love and Logic adult does not pay. One mother of a particularly difficult teenager put it this way:

Once in a while Conner will try to pull something over on me. It's like he needs a little "tune up" from time to time. But now I know how to make sure he regrets his poor decisions. And the great part is that the empathy keeps me the good guy.

During one of his mother's lie-related work slow-downs, Conner asked her, "How come you're making such a big deal out of this? How come on the news all them politicians and business guys get to lie?"

Like a true master of Love and Logic, she hugged him, smiled warmly, and answered:

I guess those guys just didn't have great mommas like yours.

Creativity in Children
By Foster W. Cline, M.D.
Vol. 19, No. 1

Want to be a happy mama and papa? Raise children who are creative. Of course, creativity has to be combined with self-discipline. If you have a creative child who has no self-discipline, then you have raised "the child from hell." After all, it is creative to paint on the walls, color the dog with nail polish, and shoot colored ink onto the ceiling with a water pistol. Self-discipline and creativity are not related and are independent variables. Self-disciplined children can be either creative or not. And creative children can be self-disciplined or not. As a parent, shoot for both!

Lucky is the parent who has a creative child. Why? Because truly creative children are *self-stimulating*. They are motivated to accomplish on their own. Creativity is a *doing* concept. No one can be creative while watching a football game or watching TV. Creative children don't whine, "What can I do?" and "What can I watch?"

Encouraging Creativity in Early Toddlerhood

Creativity is strongly related to inquisitiveness. Toddlerhood is *the* most important time for a parent to encourage their child's curiosity. During these foundation years, the brain is very malleable and its growth is completely dependent on environmental givens and expectations. Amazingly, the brain is physically changed by what takes place during infancy and todderhood.

Ages two to six are the ages of industry and initiative. Wise parents encourage their children to explore the environment. Unhappily, I often see toddlers exploring the environment in airport waiting areas or in the church vestibule, not bothering anybody, and I see parents discouraging the children by saying, "Come here" when the children aren't going anyplace anyway. I feel sorry for both the children and the parents. Let the kids go. Let them explore. As long as they are not intruding on another's space or tranquility, relax!

During toddlerhood wise parents excite their children by showing enthusiasm about exploring and understanding the world: "What makes that go around?" And, "Wow, when that gets hot, it bubbles." Toddlers love learning how to work the buttons on the DVD player and the TV. They want to know how high they can stack pebbles; how cream mixes with coffee when it is stirred. Wise parents are forever saying, "Wow, look at that! How does that work?"

144

Discipline, as I said above, is an essential element for happiness with the curious child. Only discipline leads to a joyful exploring of the environment that is fun for both parent and child. It's only enjoyable to have toddlers explore in the waiting room or church vestibule if they will come when called; only fun to have children watch how coffee mixes with cream if they respect the adult's wishes that they not grab the cup. I was recently in a home in which the kids were designing the Snake River Drainage Basin all over the kitchen floor. I asked the young mom about the watery mess the kids were making in front of refrigerator and stove, and she laughed, saying, "Well, the kitchen floor is made to be wet. And it works because they clean it up as soon as I ask!"

Encouraging Creativity in Early Childhood

The easiest "no-brainer" way to encourage creativity in early childhood is to deep-six the TV. But that's almost impossible for young parents who themselves grew up with TV in their formative years. But it is probably sufficient to say that all children should spend more time *doing* something at home than *watching* something. The following is a partial list, which could be endless, of how parents have encouraged creativity in early childhood:

- Use a thrift shop as your toy store, and buy clocks and all sorts of mechanical stuff to take apart, clothes for dress-up, and old jewelry boxes to store and collect important stuff. Start your child's collection of old postcards, salt and pepper shakers, and padlocks.
- Make sure you have a white wall covered with plastic for dry-marker drawings. Ideally, every home is built with a few secret places for kids to hide and put their treasures. Every home would be better off with a built-in stage than a built-in media center.
- In addition to reading stories to your children, make up stories, round-robin fashion.
- Make sure, as in Mary Poppins style, that every job has an element of fun. In early childhood, there should always be three elements to washing dishes, making beds, and cleaning

the bathroom: you, the kid, and fun! When the child is six or seven, you take one step backwards, and the child is left with the job and the fun. My son, coming home from college, while doing the dishes, remarked, "Dad, when I do the dishes, I still hear the germs scream as I wash them down the drain!"

Encouraging Creativity in Childhood
Childhood is the time when the entrepreneurs and inventors of the future really start to bloom. Parents encourage this by showing excitement around their child's areas of strength. These are the years of exposure to the wonders of the world. Exposure to museums, art shows, plays, and dinner theaters. Whatever the child is exposed to, it is most effective only if the parent is excited about the experience, too. Whatever activity the parents experience with joy, in the company of their children, the children take up with relish and after a time usually become self-absorbed in it without parental input. My own mom interested my brother and me in darkrooms, guppy breeding, butterfly collecting, and writing by being excited about all these activities for a short time, before turning the darkroom, aquariums, butterfly nets, and manuscript submissions over to us. Her motto was, "Try it, you'll probably like it!" And her love coupled with her excited curiosity about the world has lasted us for three-quarters of a century.

In summary, show excitement about how things work, do things with your children, become excited about what they, and you, discover, and you will probably raise a self-motivated, curious, and creative child.

© 2003 Foster W. Cline, M.D.

Broken Agreements
By Jim Fay
Vol. 19, No. 2

Mom is faced with a dilemma. She entered into an agreement with Sarah, her seventeen-year-old-daughter, that she would allow her to buy her own car provided no other teenagers rode with her until she was eighteen years of age.

One of Mom's friends witnessed Sarah driving with other kids in the car and reported it. Now that Mom has evidence that the agreement was broken, she is concerned about addressing this with her daughter.

Her concerns are related to several issues: Sarah now owns the car, Mom did not see the violation herself, and she has concerns about enforcing the agreement and basing it on the word of other adults in the community.

I am suggesting that she handle this with a discussion with Sarah, followed by some action that enforces the agreement. The following is predictive of the way these conversations often go:

MOM: "Sarah, you had someone riding with you. Our agreement was that you could have and drive the car, as long as there were no other kids riding with you during the first year. You broke our contract."

SARAH: "I didn't have anyone else in the car. What do you mean?"

MOM: "Now we have a broken contract and a lie. That's making it worse."

SARAH: "How do you know that? Who told you that? Have you been spying on me? Don't you trust me? I want to know who's been ratting me out."

MOM: "I'm your parent. It's my job to know what's going on."

SARAH: "But you didn't see me driving with other kids. This is so stupid!"

MOM: "Did our agreement say you couldn't have other riders, or did it say that you could have them as long as you didn't get caught?"

SARAH: "But Mom, that rule was so lame in the first place. So what's the big deal anyway? What's a car for if you can't take your friends places? Besides, it's my car. I paid for it. You have no business telling me what I can do with it. None of my friends get treated like babies."

Mom: "So I didn't hear the answer to my question. What was our agreement?"

Sarah: "I don't care about that stupid agreement. I paid for the car and you're not making any more rules about it. Get off my case."

Mom: "Our agreement was that you could have and drive the car, as long as no other teens are with you. You broke the agreement and I'm going to have to do something about it."

Sarah: "Well you better not take my car. You can't do that. It's my property. I earned the money for it. You can just stuff your stupid rule. It's not like I'm driving drunk. I'm a good kid. I get good grades. It's not like I'm some low-life geek."

Sarah's Defense

Sarah's argument that she gets good grades and is not on drugs is a common ploy among today's teenagers. The trouble with this argument is that it so often works with parents who are confused about their role and responsibilities in raising kids. But it's not enough to just raise a kid who gets good grades and doesn't drink or do drugs. The parenting job also includes raising kids who are honest, considerate, respectful, responsible, and have good character.

Sarah, like many lawyers, has created a defense for breaking the rules and lying. How would it sound if she presented the following defense to the court?

Your Honor, my client is a good girl. Look at her good report cards. That alone should prove it. But you also need to know that she is not a drunk, druggy, or a low-life geek.

Now, as to this minor issue about breaking her contract and lying about it, the court has no business even considering sanctions against my client when there are other teenagers who do much worse things. The court should simply appreciate the opportunity to work with such an outstanding young person.

And, Your Honor, the plaintiff did not see her daughter break the contract. The only way this contract could possibly be valid is if the plaintiff actually sees, with her own eyes, the rules of the agreement being violated. The eyewitness accounts of this violation do not apply in this case.

And there is an additional reason to find my client not guilty. She had to agree to her mother's lame rules in order to be allowed to buy the car. Most kids don't have to do this. Their parents even buy their cars for them.

In other words, my client was coerced into agreeing to a contract that should, in fact, be null and void by the nature of its unreasonable demands. My poor client had to sign the agreement under duress, and therefore, should be excused and found not guilty.

And, as if that is not enough, my client paid for the car with her own money. It is now her property to do with as she pleases. The plaintiff in this matter has absolutely no rights to tell her how to use her own property. The court has no other choice than to find my client not guilty. Thank you.

We know that a judge would laugh this case right out of court. The defense that only bad people should be held accountable for their actions doesn't stand up in our justice system. And it should never stand up in a family.

The Personal Property Issue

I agree that the car is, in fact, the property of Sarah. Mom agreed that she could own a car. However, as it is with all of the other possessions Sarah owns, Mom still has a responsibility to place limits on their use. The fact that Sarah owns a bow and arrow set does not mean that she can use it in unsafe ways. Sarah's ownership of a computer does not give her total control over its use. The same is true of the car.

Mom Takes Action

Based on all of this, Mom took action. She did not take the car away. Remember that Sarah told her that the car was hers and

Mom could not take it away. So, this wise mother did the next best thing. She purchased a club for the steering wheel of Sarah's car and locked it into place. Sarah discovered the locked steering wheel and was furious. "Mom! This is so stupid! You have no right! You get that off my steering wheel right now! I don't have to put up with this! This is my car!"

"Yes, Sweetie. It is your car and I won't take it away from you. You have the right to own it. I'm your parent and I have the responsibility to decide when you drive it. I'll take that off your steering wheel the day that I no longer worry about how you use the car. I'm living up to my end of the bargain that we both made."

Needless to say, there was a major teen temper tantrum followed by much pouting and grumbling. But Mom stuck to her guns and two weeks later the two of them created a new agreement.

We all need to give Mom a pat on the back for not being afraid to be a real parent. It's the Love and Logic way.

© 2003 Jim Fay

"Big Boys Do It in the Potty" ... and Other Adventures: How to Get Your Toddler to Do Just About Anything You Want
By Charles Fay, Ph.D.

Vol. 19, No. 2

There's got to be a magic bullet for taming toddlers and getting them to do what you want! How do you get those little kiddos to brush their teeth, pick up their toys, use the potty, or anything else?

I saw some marvelous clues to this age-old question, watching a small boy ... no more than three years old ... picking up trash in a large room I was speaking in. My audience had left for the lunch hour, and there I sat, eating my sandwich and marveling at this tiny dynamo. I couldn't help but stare at what was happening! There he was, toddling from aisle to aisle, picking up empty coffee cups, gum wrappers, scraps of paper, and other refuse.

There was no doubt in my mind that I had finally found the perfect employee. He had it all ... enthusiasm, energy, and an apparently unbridled desire to please. I found myself wondering, "How could such a small child be motivated to work so much harder than many of the teenagers ... and some of the adults ... I've known?"

There had to be an explanation! Was he being threatened with loss of life or limb? The smile on his face suggested no. Was he being highly compensated with copious amounts of candy or cash? I doubted this, as well.

The answer to this puzzle walked just a few steps ahead. There she was ... Grandma! She was wonderful and wise, smiling back at him as they worked together. Grandma volunteered in that church auditorium almost every day, making it gleam for all to enjoy. Most days, little Cory came along to "help" for an hour or two.

From years of raising good kids, Grandma had learned the secret formula for getting kids to do what she wanted. The ingredients didn't involve threats, and they didn't involve punishments. There were no goodies promised either.

Grandma knew in her heart that the single most powerful way of getting a child to brush their teeth, do chores, eat vegetables, use the potty ... or anything else ... was to model it with great excitement and joy. She learned long ago that little kids want to be big like their parents. She also learned that little kids who have fun doing "big people chores" with their parents and grandparents grow into teenagers and adults who are fun to be around ... and don't bicker and complain about helping around the house.

The single most powerful way of getting a child to brush their teeth, do chores, eat vegetables, use the potty ... or anything else ... is to model it with great excitement and joy.

In our work with thousands of parents, we've noticed that the most successful ones are constantly doing the things they want their kids to do ... when they know their kids are watching.

Experiment with this:
When your kids are watching, be silly and
sing a song as you are brushing your teeth,
combing your hair, picking up
your clothes, etc.
It worked for Snow White!

Watching Grandma, I couldn't help but ponder over the power of teaching by example. It's an old concept, but one that's too darn easy to forget. It can also be sort of a bummer, since it means that we actually have to behave!

Watching Grandma, I also couldn't help but notice how she intuitively understood the research done by Albert Bandura in the 1960s and 1970s. While she didn't have a Ph.D., and had never studied this research, Grandma "knew" that kids are much more likely to copy adults who are:

Loving

There was no doubt that Grandma and Cory were attached at the hip! It doesn't take research to know that kids copy people they like, love, or respect. A simple rule of great parenting is to have lots and lots of fun with our kids when they are behaving, so they feel emotionally bonded to us. This all-powerful attachment serves as the catalyst for modeling process.

Since this bond is typically a bit less tumultuous when our children are tiny, might it not be wise to start modeling as early as possible?

Patient

From time to time, Cory would try to throw away something he shouldn't. Toddling behind Grandma, he'd occasionally try to throw away someone's notebook, purse, or something else he shouldn't. Instead of getting angry, Grandma would smile and sing with glee, "Silly! That is so silly! That doesn't go in the trash!" Then she'd simply put the item back.

It wasn't long before Cory was doing the same. Looking at a purse, he smiled, pointed, and sang, "Silly! That not trash! Silly!"

Isn't it sad that so many young children lose their love of helping when the adults around them get frustrated and angry?

Viewed by the child as similar to themselves

For years, the research on modeling, or "observational learning," has told us that kids are much more likely to model after someone they perceive as similar to themselves. Here's the dilemma: In what way did little Cory view his grandma as similar to himself?

Working in the schools, I've seen wonderful instance after instance of kids bonding with, and modeling after, adults from very different ethnic, cultural, or religious backgrounds from themselves. In each of these instances, the teacher created a perception of similarity by noticing unique qualities and interests of these kids. Isn't it interesting that we tend to see people who care about us as being more similar to ourselves than those we view as cold or distant?

Experiment with this:
At least twice a week, smile and whisper to your child,
"I noticed that you _____."
Fill in the blank with something very unique about
your child or something that they really like.

Powerful

Do kids respect and model after adults who act like doormats? Of course not! We tend to copy people we view as caring yet strong at the same time. Might this explain why parents who set firm yet loving limits have youngsters who are much more likely to become firm yet loving adults?

Seen by the child as being rewarded by the behavior performed

Bandura observed that children were far more likely to copy a behavior if the person performing it was rewarded in some way. While no one was handing Grandma goodies for tidying the room, something even more powerful was happening: From time to time, she would pause, smile at Cory, and say, "This is so much fun! I love cleaning. It makes me feel so proud!"

Grandma was rewarding herself, and her little grandson was soaking it up, too.

Experiment with this:
As you are doing chores in front of your kids,
reading, volunteering, etc., smile from time to time and
talk about how proud you feel when the job is done.

Less than perfect but always improving

Here's the best news of all. We tend to copy people we see as being less than perfect! Isn't it nice to know that sometimes it's good to make mistakes in front of our kids? When adults try too hard to be perfect, their kids probably see it as impossible to live up to such immaculate examples.

I'll never forget the day my father came home and described in great detail how he'd forgotten to turn off his wireless microphone during a bathroom break. He made that mistake so I didn't have to. Thanks, Dad!

Never underestimate the power of modeling.

A mother attending one of my parenting courses pulled me aside after the final class. Smiling from ear to ear, she said something like:

I thought you were a total freak! When you told me to model using the potty for my son, I thought you were crazy ... especially when you said to make it fun by singing and being silly. How gross. But it worked, and it was easy. I just kept acting really excited when I was sitting there and telling him that he couldn't use the potty because "it was only for big boys ... that big boys do it in the potty ... and that using the potty is too much fun for little ones." After about three weeks, I heard him screaming from the bathroom. There he was, singing and carrying on. I couldn't believe it!

Have fun with your kids, and have fun modeling the joy life has to offer.

© 2003 Charles Fay, Ph.D.

Love and Logic Also Works on Our Elderly Parents
By Foster W. Cline, M.D.
VOL. 19, NO. 2

How often have you heard us at Love and Logic say, "Remember, someday your children may be choosing your nursing home"? Well, some of us are now at the point in our lives where we indeed need to face that task. As our parents age, we are involved in making decisions about their life and living situation. Roles are reversed, and we are the competent ones usually returning, for better or worse, the type of love, affection, and care they long ago gave us. This is also a good time to ask ourselves, "What should I be doing to ensure that my children and grandchildren will visit me when I get to that time of my life?"

At this point in our lives our Love and Logic training really needs to kick in. It is essential that we give our elderly parents choices when possible. It is also important that they feel they have some control over their lives. For instance, when independent living becomes problematic for our parents, their basic options are usually:

a. Living with us or near us with or without home care.
b. Placement in an independent living facility.
c. Placement in a licensed care facility.

There are important issues to consider in each of these situations. And this short article can't examine all of them. But a short list of items to look for in care facilities is given below.

Regardless of how we are involved, and the decisions that are made, we must always keep in mind the primary issue: "Are the decisions that I'm attempting to make, or help with, increasing the quality of life for my parents and for me and my family?"

Now this may seem obvious, but it isn't. Over and over again, as a physician, I have seen grown children visit their parents in care facilities out of a misguided sense of duty. The parents either don't remember that their child has been visiting them, or complain continually that the children don't visit them enough. And the visit is thoroughly unenjoyable. The grown child can leave feeling a combination of anger, guilt, and resentment. And the parents, likewise, feel no more relaxed or satisfied because of the visit. It is a wise child who may say to their parents, "Mom/Dad, if I find that visiting you doesn't make me and you happier, there is no reason for the visit." Why do children visit parents when neither feels more joy following the visit? Perhaps it is because some children consciously or unconsciously may believe, "My parent put up with me when I raised hell, so it's only right that now it's my turn to take it."

Our aging parents have combinations of three situations: aging or loss of mind with functional body; loss of body functions with functioning mind; and loss of mind and body. In the cases where the mind is not functioning well, or may not be functioning well shortly, it is essential to have a general or at least limited power of attorney. And in any case, it is essential to have the numbers of the parent's neighbors, physicians, attorneys, and accountants before an acute illness or emergency strikes.

Parents usually appreciate an up-front approach concerning the plans for their final resting place or internment. Many parents make these arrangements in advance to spare the children the necessity of making them during a time of grief.

If our parent's mind is functioning near normally, and body is failing, we may feel like laying down the options and telling our parent what to do. However, this is the road to family estrangement. As with children, Love and Logic teaches that we have to be very careful about attempting to control another person. We have to express our opinion without orders. For instance, we can't say, "Mom, living alone is no longer an option," but we generally must be content to say, "Living alone may no longer be a good option. Let's look at some of the choices available." Attempting to force a parent with a functioning mind into an independent living facility or extended care facility almost always pulls families apart, and is the source for a great deal of hard feelings. Thankfully, when most folks need more intense care, they themselves realize it. It is very important to remember that we must include them in the decision making. There may be some issues that we feel are essential but they do not. We must keep their well-being *and* their social and other interests in mind.

There are a number of ways to evaluate a facility:

- Visit the rehabilitation facilities. This is very important.
- Eat a meal at the facility.
- Take a walk through the facility during swing and night shifts.
- It is absolutely essential to talk to the residents about their satisfaction or dissatisfaction with the facility.
- Check turnover of the certified nursing assistants (CNAs).
- What are the activities for the week?
- How big and well kept are the outside safety gardens? Are they safe for the wandering and confused residents?
- How are pets handled.
- Does the facility offer private rooms or require roommates? If residents must share rooms, how easy is it to change roommates in situations of incompatibility?
- Is in-home care available and how easy is it to flow between levels of care when and if physical or mental changes do take place?

Laws are changing, and care facilities are being required by government to do more with less and less. Responsibilities, paperwork, and expectations are raised as funding is cut. The federal privacy rules make clear and loving communication within many facilities problematic. When you hear "201A needs help getting to dinner," just remember that every home in the world would rather say, "'Mr. Smith' or 'John' needs some help getting to dinner." But federal privacy rules won't allow it.

This makes it increasingly important for us to make sure that we give our aging parents the love, respect, and attention that they gave us when we were growing up. We need to make sure that we visit them and include them in family traditions. If they can no longer leave the facility, bring the celebration to them.

I heard of one young bride who knew that her grandmother would not be able to attend her wedding. It was very important to her that her grandmother be part of the celebration. Her solution: She decided to break tradition and let her groom see her before she walked down the aisle. The bride made arrangements with the management of the facility where her grandmother was living to have not only her grandmother, but all of the residents, meet in the main dining area. The bride, groom, and all of the attendants went to the facility a few hours before they needed to be at the church and spent time with her grandmother and all of her friends. The management reported that this act of kindness, consideration, and love by the young bride and groom made a world of difference for all of those living at the facility. No one had ever done this for them before and they talked about it for months.

Just as we use Love and Logic with our children as they are growing up, it is a great teaching experience for our children and grandchildren to see us using Love and Logic with our elderly parents and grandparents. What great modeling. And remember ... someday your children may be choosing *your* nursing home.

© *2003 Foster W. Cline, M.D.*

If You Can, They Can: Learning to Handle Life's Bumps and Bruises
By Jim Fay
VOL. 19, NO. 3

Little Sara was visibly nervous as she waited for the doctor, but seemed to be holding up reasonably well. She would visit her new pediatrician. The doctor, a cheerful man with a warm personality, came out to meet her: "Hi, Sara, follow me and we'll get that finger fixed up. It'll be easy, won't hurt at all." With that he spun on his heals and headed for his office.

Psychological studies have taught us that kids take their emotional cues from the adults in their lives. If the parent is concerned, those feelings transfer to the kids, and if the parent is confident, the child feels more secure. We also know that these feelings are transferred more through tone of voice and body language than they are through words.

Being well versed in this fact of human nature, I was not surprised to see Sara throw back her shoulders and start to follow the doctor. But alas, Mom blew it. In the most sincere, concerned, whiny voice, dripping with concern, she said, "It'll be okay. You don't have to worry."

You don't have to be a clinical wizard to know what happened next. This confident-looking little child turned and raced back to her Mom. She was instantly transformed from a bold child to a Velcro child, clinging to her mother. At this point, the situation deteriorated as Mom became even more reassuring: "Now you don't have to be afraid, I'll be right here. He's a nice man. It won't hurt."

There was no need for this. All Mom had to do was follow Sara down the hallway and not say a word. Sara was doing just fine. But guess who wasn't. Mom had concerns and passed them on with her attempts at reassurance. Kids are unbelievably sensitive to their parents' emotions. So as soon as Sara heard the concern oozing out of her mother's voice, she knew that trouble was on the way. Mom's words said one thing, but her voice said something else. Kids have finely tuned antennae. They listen more to the tone of voice than the words.

I worked in schools for thirty-one years. I saw two different kinds of parents dropping off their kids each morning. There were the parents who bid their kids goodbye with: "Lucky you! You get to spend the day with the other kids. Hope you have a great day! See you later, pal." These moms and dads would spin on their heels and race back to their cars. Both their words and their tone of voice were in sync, saying, "I can handle this, so can you." As you can guess, their kids would race off to class.

The other parents became famous to the school staff. Their kids would hang on to them, needing three or four hugs: "Go now. I can't stay with you. You've got to learn to do this on your own. I don't have time for this. No, I'm not going to walk to class with you. What is the matter with you? Okay, one more hug and then I have to go."

Even when these parents walk off, their body language is different. There is no spring in their stride. To make things worse, they turn to see if their child is heading for the school, and the second they turn, the kid races back and the scene starts all over again. Their words say, "Go," and their tone of voice and body language says, "I'm not sure either of us can handle this."

Any experienced teacher can tell you that once these kids are pried off the parent and enter the classroom, it only takes a few seconds before they are happy.

The Solution

To solve this problem we helped the moms understand several things:

1. The kids were happy once the parent left.
2. It is normal for loving parents to feel conflicted about their kids being away from them.
3. It is not selfish to send school-age kids off to be with their friends and teachers.
4. The problem is more with the parent than with the child. It's difficult to get kids to outperform their adult role models.
5. These parents need to come across to the children in a different way. They need to show their children that they can easily handle leaving them at school.

This required the moms to learn how to talk about school with their kids in a new and different way: Quit talking to the children like babies, and pretend that they are other adults.

The problem was usually solved once the parent learned to say the following in a very upbeat, confident way:

You know, pal, I love being with you before and after school. That's what being a mom is all about. I just figured out that it's no fun having you around during school hours. That's my time to do adult things, so I decided that since it's no fun having you around during school hours, the fun will start for me again when you come home. That's our time together. So, off you go!

Some readers might have a difficult time reading this. They would say, "How can you be so harsh or rejecting to a child?" Our experience tells us that there are two kinds of parents who might think this way. The first are the people who don't need to talk like this because of good emotional health. They provide loving boundaries. They know it and their kids know it. This person can't even imagine needing to talk like this. Their words, voice, and body language are all congruent

The second kind of parent might think this technique is unloving. These are the people who *really* need to learn to set healthy and loving boundaries. There is an old rule in psychology that says, "People who can easily use a technique seldom need to. But people who don't think they can use this approach *desperately need to.*"

Once when our neighbors were visiting, four-year-old Amos was crawling under our heavy iron table. Pow! He stood up and banged his head on the table. "Ouch!" I thought. "That's really going to hurt." What a temptation if was for all of us to descend on Amos and lather him with sympathy.

There was a moment of dead silence. Amos turned and stared at his parents. It was as if he was looking for a clue about how bad this was. "Kaboomer!" said Dad with enthusiasm. "Rub it hard. It'll be okay!" exclaimed Mom.

Amos rubbed his head, smiled, and walked away. His Mom called to him and said, "It's a good thing you're tough. Probably don't want to do that again. Go play and have a good time."

As he left, the parents talked about their new way of handling their kids' bumps and bruises. "We used to make a big deal about these things. Seeing our kids fall seemed to hurt us more than it did the kids. We found out that our kids fell apart when we fell apart. The more upset we became about their little hurts, the less they were able to handle them."

These wise parents discovered that if they wanted their kids to toughen up, they had to be the models for that. That doesn't mean that they're uncaring and callous. They don't tell their kids not to cry. Dad told me that they often find themselves saying, "I know that hurts. A little hug might make it better." The important thing is that their tone of voice tells the kids that they can handle what life dishes out.

Spend a little time this week imagining what you want your kids to be like as adults. Then model that behavior. Remember that kids don't learn from being told, they learn by being shown. You are the most important role model in your kids' life.

© 2003 Jim Fay

Love and Logic Thoughts on Therapy
By Foster W. Cline, M.D.
VOL. 19, NO. 3

My child has behavior problems. Do I need a therapist? When is Love and Logic not useful?

Love and Logic is *always* useful. In the most difficult of situations Love and Logic helps everyone keep their sanity. For instance, the Love and Logic tools of problem separation, taking good care of yourself, using consequences with empathy rather than punishment, and using encouragement rather than praise are applicable in all situations. However, sometimes Love and Logic needs to be augmented by other therapeutic techniques or counseling. Simply having an outside point of view may be helpful. Sometimes the ubiquitous psychological atmosphere of our home conceals how we may be contributing to problems, because, after all, something that is present everywhere is hard to see anywhere.

If the principles of Love and Logic are known and have been used to the best of the parent's ability, and there is no definite improvement within eight weeks or so, a therapist should be sought. However, remember that when a family who has never used Love and Logic begins using it, things may temporarily get worse before they get better. Children may resist taking responsibility for their behavior. At first they may prefer the old rant, rave, and rescue routine over consequences with empathy. Change takes time. Most parents report immediate improvement when using Love and Logic techniques. They can hardly wait to report, week-by-week, even day-by-day, the changes they see. But this is not always the case when parents and children are coping with deeper issues of depression, developmental delays, or neurologic deficits. Medication helps many problems that are driven by the brain, *not* management of mind and heart.

In this short article, I cannot list all of the problems that could call for a therapist. A few common ones are: frequent rage reactions secondary to an infancy disturbed by frequent moves, surgery, or abuse and neglect; rage reactions in which the child feels both remorseful but unable to maintain self-control; and bipolar problems, severe ADD, and neurologic and developmental disorders. Sometimes temporal lobe seizures and head trauma call for good diagnostic workup and probably will be helped by medication.

Most problems that call for medication are apparent by toddlerhood. However, childhood depression, schizophrenia, and bipolar problems may appear first in the teen years. Often there is a family history of such problems.

Sudden and *marked* changes in a child's or teen's demeanor almost always call for therapeutic consultation. Such is the case when a strong and happy family, with loving and respectful children, suddenly experiences a child who becomes distant, lets their achievement drop, or becomes downright negative and disrespectful. When a loving, high-achieving young teen daughter suddenly becomes angry and does unimaginable things such as stealing the parent's credit card and going on spending sprees, then bipolar problems must be suspected. Usually the shocked parents, and even professionals, may first accuse the child of drug use, which the child always angrily and vehemently denies.

How Do I Choose a Therapist?

Every profession harbors a population of "certified" folks who are not at all helpful or give bad advice. Complicating this issue is the fact that many therapists carry psychological baggage of their own from unhappy or dysfunctional childhoods. One only needs to go to the nearest high school to ask the seniors, "Which of you wants to become a therapist?" to see the children with disturbed backgrounds raise their hands. The baggage that these therapists carry is inevitably laid upon the unsuspecting clients.

And response from a therapist is difficult to evaluate. When you get bad advice from your contractor, it is a no-brainer to see that the dormers leak or the walls aren't true. When you get bad investment advice, it shows only too clearly in your portfolio. However, except for the prescription of medication, it is almost impossible for a family to measure the value of the therapy. Therapy may go on for months (or even years!) with no improvement, but the family keeps paying for the therapy because:

- They know that things take time.
- The therapist says he or she sees improvement in the child.
- They believe that they are continuing to do something wrong, or are not being responsive enough.
- They don't want to expect too much!

In short, when there is no improvement, the therapist is in a good position to get off scot-free.

So how do you find a good therapist? Looking through the yellow pages is not nearly as effective as going to a professional who definitely helped a friend's family. Most good therapists have good reputations. They are not usually unknown individuals. I have found that most therapists who give solid advice live solid lives themselves. If I wanted to get advice on children, I would go to a therapist who has loving children who are responsible and respectful. If I needed marriage therapy, I would to go to a therapist who has been happily married for years. In summary, I don't want a poverty-stricken investment counselor! We all do best with a professional who walks-the-walk, not simply talks-the-talk.

A little research can go a long way. Most state medical societies keep databases of physicians on the Internet. These are available to all consumers. If there have been problems in a physician's past, they often show up. Most head nurses in a child psychiatric unit will tell you who are the really effective psychologists and psychiatrists.

If you search around and one or another professional's name keeps cropping up as being helpful and responsive, there is a good chance that such a person could help you.

© 2003 Foster W. Cline, M.D.

"I Just Want My Kids to Be Happy"
By Jim Fay
VOL. 19, No. 4

How many times have you heard, "I don't care what my child does in his life, I just want him to be happy"?

Do you want your kids to have happiness for the short term, or for the long term? Here are some questions that will help you discover if you are preparing your kids for a lifetime of happiness or a lifetime of frustration:

1. Do you view frustration and struggle as potentially damaging to your child's self-concept?
2. Do you believe that kids need to do their fair share of the family chores?
3. Is your child's immediate happiness a high priority?
4. Are you willing to allow your children to be unhappy with you when they don't get their way?

5. Is it important to you that your kids are never inconvenienced or uncomfortable?

6. Do you believe that kids take better care of possessions that they have earned?

7. Do you believe that giving your kids the things you never had will make them love you more, and therefore provide long-term happiness?

8. Do you believe that achievement born out of effort and struggle is most valuable?

9. Do you believe that it is better for kids to wait until they leave the home to learn to struggle and earn what they want in life?

10. Do you believe that kids learn about the benefits of struggle and responsibility best through experience?

11. Do you believe that parents are responsible for their children's happiness?

12. Do you believe that having to wait for and earn things is good practice for the adult world?

13. Do you believe that kids learn about the benefits of effort and responsibility by being told and lectured?

If you answered yes to the even-numbered questions, you have a good chance of raising children who are better prepared for a happier adult life.

If you answered yes to the uneven-numbered questions, the odds are very high that you are raising a child who believes that it is the parent's job to treat them like royalty. These are children who are positive in the beliefs that their parents can, and should, solve the problems that the child creates. Their birthright entitles them to have what they want, when they want it, without having to work for it.

A lifetime of chronic unhappiness awaits these children. It is very difficult for these kids to look to their own behaviors, decisions, or lack of effort as the source of their problems. Once they see themselves as a victim, chronic unhappiness sets in. These feelings can continue for life, because their expectations of how others should treat them or provide for them are seldom met. They have been given a prescription for unhappiness. In their eyes, everything that goes wrong is someone else's fault or just the result of bad luck.

We all know friends and neighbors who create children like this by working hard to provide immediate happiness for them. Their kids have the best and latest toys and gadgets. These parents are quick to blame and attack anyone who gets in the way of their children's happiness.

Teachers often experience the wrath of these parents when grades are less than perfect. When things go wrong at school, the parents' question to the child is seldom, "What did you do wrong?" or "Did you fail to put out enough effort?" Most often these parents are asking, "What's wrong with the teacher?" or "What's wrong with the school?"

It is not uncommon for these parents to lie for their children and to do their school projects. They love their children and do everything they can to manufacture a perfect life for them. Their familiar battle cry is, "I want my children to know that I will protect them, regardless of the situation."

Children in these homes live like honored guests. They seldom do their fair share of the work to keep the home and family running well, but are quick to blame their parents for any unhappiness. The parents are often overwhelmed with responsibilities, one of which is to provide more and more luxuries for their offspring. I have often known these children to say, "My parents 'borned' me, and it's their job to buy great stuff for me."

These parents are usually good people with a strong sense of responsibility to guarantee a happy life for their kids. But you and I have seen this family pattern over and over throughout our lives. And alas, have we ever seen it work out well in the long run?

These parents, who work so hard to provide a happy life, raise offspring who are chronically unhappy. They feel entitled to the good life without having to work for it. If you haven't seen this in your own neighborhood with your own two eyes, you might be inclined to think that I'm exaggerating. But am I?

The growth of this syndrome is a major concern to the authors of Love and Logic. If this trend continues it is possible that it could reach epidemic proportions. It is scary to consider the impact it could have on our national economy.

Do you ever wonder why television commercials are so inane? Why is there such a focus on partying? There's a good reason. The demographic being targeted by the television industry is eighteen- to thirty-four-year-olds who are still living at home, not holding full-time jobs, but spending their parent's money.

The authors of Love and Logic often talk with the parents of these young people. It is not uncommon for us to hear, "I tell him that he needs to get a job, but he can't find the kind of job that's right for him. You know, it's not like when we were young. Actually, he's overqualified for a lot of jobs available right now. We're hoping he finds something soon. We're getting tired of having to support him. It might be different if he was willing to help us out by doing some of the work around the house. I can't understand why he is so lazy, we've always given him everything he wanted."

These parents give us the problem and the answer all in one statement. If you are unwilling to let your kids struggle, experience temporary frustrations, live with the consequence of their acts, or earn what they get, then you are giving them immediate short-term happiness along with a prescription for a lifetime of chronic unhappiness.

Raising kids the Love and Logic way gives them a real advantage over others when they grow up. These kids learn that they are responsible for their own happiness. We at Love and Logic are here to help you make this happen.

© 2004 Jim Fay

Give Your Kids the Gift of Wise Money Management: Raise Kids Who'll Grow Up to Miss *You* ... Rather Than Your Money

By Charles Fay, Ph.D.

VOL. 19, NO. 4

What's the secret to raising kids who are careful with their cash? What can parents do to create children who grow up to be wise money managers? In my travels around the country, I meet two types of parents. When describing their college-age offspring, one type furls their eyebrows, wrings the hands, and ponders, "Why does money slip through his fingers like water down the drain? We constantly have to transfer money into his checking account. What's wrong with this kid?"

We meet another type of parent who beams with pride as they describe their college-age kid: "We're so proud! It's amazing how he manages to stretch his cash!"

What have we learned from this second type of parent? Listed below are some powerful yet practical tips for giving your children the gift of financial responsibility.

Start teaching your kids to save as soon as they are old enough to eat cookies.

What do cookies and cash have in common? First, both are pretty nice to have. Second, most of us can attest to the fact that both vanish quickly when self-control is lacking!

Children younger than four or five typically have difficulty truly understanding the abstract nature of money. Obviously, few young children have difficulty understanding the very concrete fact that cookies, candies, and other treats taste good.

Parents of young children can give their youngsters a head start on financial wisdom by providing an "allowance" of treats on a regular basis. One couple started by giving Toby, their three-year-old, a small stack of graham crackers on a twice-weekly basis. The graham crackers came only on Saturday and Wednesday mornings ... and there was always the same small number. When they were all gone, they were all gone. No amount of whining, begging, crying, or screaming could make Mom or Dad provide more.

Follow Love and Logic's "Four Steps to Responsibility."

Step One: Give the child a task he or she can handle. When it comes to teaching kids responsible money management, the first step involves giving them some type of allowance or "practice money" each week. With younger children, an "allowance" of cookies works better than money.

Step Two: Hope and pray the child blows it. Most folks agree that it's better for a child to learn money management by eating their cookies too fast at age three than spending their paycheck too fast at age thirty-three!

As we always say, the road to wisdom is paved with mistakes. Mistakes made earlier in life have the smallest price tags. Don't fall into the trap of reminding or lecturing your child at this point. Parents who do, rob their children of essential learning opportunities.

Step Three: Let empathy and logical consequences do the teaching. When Toby ate all of his crackers before "payday," did his parents get angry? *No!* Did they lecture and say, "A graham cracker saved is a graham cracker earned." *No!* Did they give in when he threw a fit? *No!*

With great sadness in their voices, they pointed to the large calendar on the refrigerator and said, "Oh Toby ... this is so sad. We give more graham crackers on Wednesday. That's two more days." Because Toby was a normal child, he threw a major fit.

Step Four: Give the same task again. The fourth step to responsibility involves avoiding the temptation to lecture, remind, or tell the child what he/she "should have" learned from the consequence.

Toby's parents just kept providing crackers on Wednesdays and Saturdays, the scheduled allowance days. Each week they noticed something interesting. Each week, his little stack of grahams lasted a bit longer.

Talk about hard work and saving within earshot of your kids.
Modeling is the most powerful teaching tool! That's why it's smart to let our kids see how hard we must work to earn and save money.

Kids shouldn't be overwhelmed with our adult problems. Nevertheless, it does them no favors to keep our financial struggles a secret. Have you ever noticed how kids seem to best remember what they think they are not supposed to hear?

One of the most powerful ways of teaching anything is to talk about it with another adult within earshot of our kids. When their kids are nearby, wise parents talk on the phone with a friend and say things like, "I'm proud of myself. I wanted to buy that new stereo, but I didn't. It was hard to resist, but I need to save money for groceries."

Wise parents take their kids to the bank with them so that their children can hear them say to the teller, "I need to put money into my saving account, so I don't spend it on something I don't need."

Smart parents take their kids to the store and think out loud, "I wonder if I *really* need this? Uh ... I'd better put it back. That's too expensive."

Note: This technique is only powerful if we resist the urge to tell our kids what they should be learning by watching and listening to us.

Re-create the Great Depression in your home.
By five or six years of age, children are ready to start receiving a small allowance of "practice money" each week. People often ask, "How much should they get?" There are no hard and fast guidelines ... with one exception:

> *It's better to err by giving them too little
> than by giving them too much!*

Children learn to manage money best when they have to scrimp and make do like our parents and grandparents did during the Great Depression of the 1930s. Children learn to waste money when their allowances are too large.

When they run out, provide empathy and suggestions ...
rather than anger or cash.

I'll never forget how my parents responded when I ran out of money. With genuine empathy, they would ask, "Oh no. What do you think you might do to earn more?"

Finding this a bit irritating, I'd mumble, "Don't know."

The rest of the conversation would move along as follows:

MOM: "Would you like some ideas?"

ME: "Sure ... what?"

MOM: "Some kids decide to ask the neighbors for odd jobs. How would that work?"

ME: "Umm?"

DAD: "Other kids decide to give their parents a bid on doing some of their parents' chores. I might consider paying you to scrub the mineral deposits off our shower. How would that work?"

ME: "Well ..."

MOM: "Some kids decide just to wait until Sunday, when their parents provide allowance."

By eleven or twelve years of age, give them a small budget
for clothing, school supplies, lunches, etc.

As children get older, they need to be given gradually greater responsibility for budgeting their cash and savings, and purchasing what they want and need.

Over the years, I've met many parents who've sat down with their older children and helped them create a budget, outlining the amount of money they will likely need to buy clothing, school supplies, meals, gasoline, music lessons, etc. After creating this simple written budget, they give their children just enough money ... on a weekly basis ... to purchase these items.

One parent commented, "Years ago, I gave my fourteen-year-old cash to purchase her school clothes. As I predicted, she blew most of it on just one expensive outfit. Then she was outraged with me when I refused to give her more. I didn't give in. She ended up having to wear a lot of old clothes that year. That was ten years ago. Now she comes home from college bragging and showing off all of the nice outfits she's found in consignment and secondhand stores. Because of Love and Logic, she's a much wiser shopper than her older sister!

A major long-term goal of Love and Logic is to raise kids who grow up and miss *us* ... rather than our *money*. Isn't it sad that some adult children only call home when they've run out of pesos?

There are few gifts we can give our children that are more valuable than knowing how to handle money wisely. Adults who lack these skills live lives full of disappointment and stress. Money can't buy happiness ... but wasting it can sure create a life of sadness!

There's good news! By following the tips listed above, there's no need for our kids to live their lives fearing the bill collector.

A good friend of mine was raised with Love and Logic. Reflecting back on her childhood, she often comments:

When we were kids, our parents always gave us what we needed ... and expected us to earn what we wanted. It seemed like we were always asking the neighbors for odd jobs. I'll never forget the summer I spent washing cars, mowing lawns, and pulling weeds. By that August, I'd earned enough for the stereo I wanted. I'll never forget the feeling of pride I felt going to the store and paying for it with my own money!

It's never too early or too late to give your kids the gift of pride!

© 2004 Charles Fay, Ph.D.

Consequences with *Pizzazz*
By Foster W. Cline, M.D.
VOL. 19, NO. 4

As adults, chances are pretty good that sooner or later we will face some tough times—be they in college, the work force, or as parents, eventually we all have to deal with situations that will test us. We all have choices as to how we wish to face these challenges. We can wring our hands and worry, worry, worry, or we can weigh the problem, confront it, take control, and believe it or not, even have a good time when dealing with challenges. Life gives us those choices and how we handle them can define what kind of person we choose to be.

Now if I personally come across a situation where I have the choice of wringing my hands and worrying over a problem or solving the problem with a little humor, I take the road of humor every time. I mean, why get an ulcer over something that you could get a chuckle out of?

Think about it, your life and your health would be so much better if you just looked for the humor. Granted this won't work in all situations, but it sure will work on many of the everyday challenges we face. And parenting is one area where a good sense of humor can take you, and your children, a long way. I mean, let's face it, if you don't laugh at some of the things your kids throw your way when they're going through some of their phases, you could really lose it. Parenting can be downright exhausting—you *need* a good sense of humor!

At Love and Logic we emphasize consequences. And consequences can sometimes be painful. But let us never forget that Love and Logic puts the pizzazz, the zip, and the fun into parenting, and into leadership in general. People use Love and Logic because it makes them feel good. Just like "a spoonful of sugar helps the medicine go down," creativity and a sense of humor helps the consequences go down.

This leads me to a great story that was recently related to me. After a workshop this wonderful lady came up to me and shared this old story about her family:

Years ago, I heard you speak. At that time my husband was very quiet; however, he did seem to have a tendency to be a real drill sergeant. When he did discipline the kids it was always more of a bark.

After hearing you speak I purchased some Love and Logic products. As we listened to the audios and watched the videos, my husband would often laugh and make comments.

Although he really seemed to like the Love and Logic philosophy, I never knew if it was hitting home with him. That is, not until one day when the whole family was driving home from a shopping trip.

The kids were raising low-grade heck and high-water in the back seat of our car when my husband really surprised me. (This was the first time I realized that he really was listening when I had all of those Love and Logic products playing.) When he spoke, he sounded just like you, Foster—it was great. As the kids were going at it in the back seat he said, "Guys, it's going to be a lot quieter in this car the last mile home because Mom and I will be the only ones in this car!"

There was a moment of deafening silence, then our ten-year-old son, in a slightly challenging and snarky voice said, "You wouldn't do that!" My husband gave me a quick wink and a devilish smile as he said to the kids, "That's what Tommy said."

Again a moment of silence, then our oldest asked, "Who's Tommy?"

My husband very seriously replied, "Why Tommy is your older brother!" The silence was deafening. The kids just looked at each other with big eyes.

Now at the time we lived out in the country and in those days you never had to worry about your kids walking home. In fact, they walked home all the time and really enjoyed it. (Of course, when they were told that they had to walk home it was a different story—all of a sudden it became pure torture.) So, my husband stopped the car a mile from home and the kids got out and hiked it.

This turned out to be a great consequence—one that really worked. In fact, we never got a chance to use the method for a second time, because our psychic space was never bothered that much again.

But the cute, and wonderful, thing is that now our kids are grown and when they travel with their families we can always count on them sending us a postcard and signing it, "Poor Lost Tommy." It's become the family joke ... Wandering Tom is still out there somewhere, roving the highways and byways of the world after being kicked out of the car and becoming lost on his way home.

So Foster, thanks to you and Love and Logic, not only did the consequence work for us all those years ago, but as you can see it has become a great source of fun for the whole family.

I think the lessons in this lady's story are clear—when the going gets tough, the tough start laughing. Laughing, joking, and loving their kids while imposing the consequence. This sets the model for the development of great coping skills.

Leaders often manage to keep their sense of humor during the tough times. Just about anyone can keep it during good times, but it takes someone with great strength and fortitude to keep it in the tough times. So when we take things seriously, yet are still able to look the beast in the eye and laugh, we generally face our monsters more effectively. And we certainly set the model of coping for our children. This is a very valuable skill, for it will help them get through those tough times that they will someday need to face.

© 2004 Foster W. Cline, M.D.

VOLUME
20

Computer Game Addiction
By Jim Fay
Vol. 20, No. 1

"How could this happen?" worried Paul's mother. She finally realized that her son had become addicted to Internet computer games. Before today she had been ambivalent about the amount of time he spent in his room playing the games, and was able to convince herself that it was not all that bad. After all, when he is off in his room they aren't arguing about things and she doesn't have to have him under foot. His interest in the computer games keeps him out of the way so she can do the things she wants to do, and provides an inexpensive baby-sitter.

Denial has great power over humans. In this case, it helped Mom avoid seeing the real problem. She even had days when she was able to think, "Other kids are out smoking dope. Other kids are out getting into trouble. How can his interest in the games be so bad? He's safe in his room; I know where he is and what he's doing." Of course, this kind of thinking makes about as much sense as, "Other kids rape and murder. My kid's not that bad. He only sells drugs."

Recently she saw a television news show that touted the millions of dollars a local school paid to provide academic instruction through computer games. The news reporter said that the kids loved the games and were actually scoring better on their school tests. This information helped her feel better about Paul's compulsive use of the computer games at home.

Paul's mom actually convinced herself that all the time he spent on the computer games was good for his self-concept. She told her friend, Mary, "You know, Paul isn't good at a lot of things other boys are good at. Now he's found something that he's good at. I just know that his self-concept will grow with his successes with the games."

But alas, Mom's thinking got a jolt. She attended a seminar on addictions. The expert talked about common addictions, such as alcohol, drugs, gambling, etc. It was a shock when the therapist talked about the devastating effects of computer addiction. She learned about the breakdown of family relationships when children or adults became consumed with their computers and lost interest in each other. Depression increased in many of these families, as well. To add to her concern she learned about documented changes in the brain experienced by those who became addicted to the games.

Mom developed new resolve to look at what she had done to her son by encouraging his infatuation with the screen and the keyboard instead of learning to relate to the family. She realized that family members had drifted apart since she had allowed the computer to take over raising her children.

It was at this time that she came to grips with the fact that her children were only learning what the computer programmers wanted them to learn, and that was to buy and play more of their games. A review of the report cards gave her another jolt. School grades were on a downhill slide.

Mom now knew that she had to take action. This was going to be difficult, since school and society provide support for children owning and using computers. Her children's high school even suggested that each student have his/her own laptop computer. It seemed that the computers were continually connected to the Internet. It did not help that Dad brought work home each night to do on his computer. How could she restrict her children's use of the computers when they saw Dad spending so much of his time that way?

"Doing something about this is not going to be easy," she thought. The seminar expert talked about children who became violent and abusive when their time on the computer was restricted. If she was going to take a stand on this issue, she needed a plan and some support.

Getting Paul's father on board was going to be important. Early in her marriage she had learned that her best chance of doing this was to lay out the facts of what she had learned without telling Dad what to do about it. She hoped that he would see this situation for the disaster that it had become.

Mom and Dad had recently attended a "Becoming a Love and Logic Parent" class. One of the most important skills they learned was how to create a plan and then shelve the plan until they could share it with others. The purpose of this was to get help identifying the holes in the plan. If other adults could see loopholes in the plan, surely a child could find a way of making the plan fail. The price of failure at this point was too great to take chances. Paul was escaping from the challenges of relating to others by living with his addiction.

Both Mom and Dad sought out the services of an addiction specialist in an attempt to understand the challenges they and their boy were going to face. The therapist helped them understand that they would soon be seeing typical behaviors of addicts. Once Paul realized that they were serious about limiting his time on the computer, the pull of his addiction would drive him to do whatever it took to regain access to the computer games.

"No," said Mom. "Paul is a good kid who has never been prone to being sneaky or defiant. He will understand that we are trying to help him." Months later she told how wrong she was about this. "When we took away his computer, he sneaked time on his dad's computer. When we put a password on dad's computer, he found a way to break the password. He went to his friend's home, lying that he was there to do homework, but instead was using his friend's machine to continue his gaming."

Paul even found a way to buy a used computer, which he hid in his room. Mom and Dad never discovered where he got the money to buy that one. They were equally surprised to learn how he was able to sneak away to the Cyber Café when he was supposed to be in school. Truancy became a major problem.

Like all similar situations, this problem got worse before it started to turn around. Fortunately, with the support of a therapist, and finally, with Paul's determination to rejoin the real world instead of the fantasy world of gaming, there was a happy ending to this story.

As Mom looks back on this problem and how it consumed her family, she relates her disappointment that she didn't learn about

Love and Logic when her children were younger. "I'm sure the fantasy world of the games had a lot to do with the fact that they provided an illusion of control for a boy who had too few choices and consequences in his real life. He was denied the opportunity to feel needed in our family. This happened when we gave up on trying to get him to do his fair share of the work around the house. The reason we gave up was because we didn't know how to get him to do chores without constant reminders and battles."

This much wiser mom continued, "I now know that Paul has an addictive personality that made it easier to slip into the gaming addiction as a way of replacing what he was not getting out of his family life. I'm sure the odds for avoiding this problem would have been much higher if we had known and used the Love and Logic process as we raised him."

Give your children a gift. Limit the time they spend with electronic entertainment to thirty minutes per day. Brain science teaches us that kids who spend more time than this are actually doing damage to brain growth and development. Kids who spend their time doing things become doers. Kids who spend their time watching become watchers. That's how the brain grows. It's your choice.

© 2004 Jim Fay

Stickers, Tokens, Points, and Pizza Parties: Some Thoughts on the Use of Tangible Rewards
By Charles Fay, Ph.D.

VOL. 20, NO. 1

Among educators and parenting experts, few battles have been fiercer than the one waged over the use of rewards. As a college and graduate student, I found my head spinning as I read convincing arguments and research from experts on both sides of the debate. Depending on the semester, the professors I had at the time, the specific positions of Mars and Jupiter, and the barometric pressure, I found myself wavering between two extremist groups.

There were semesters when I found myself aligning with the "anti-reward activists." These folks cited convincing research proposing that we should never use rewards with kids. Still strong in their beliefs today, this group holds that rewards cause kids to lose self-motivation and to become addicted to external controls. Folks in this camp often argue that rewards are manipulative or coercive.

As planetary alignments changed, I'd find myself attracted to the "sticker commando" camp. These folks cited convincing studies suggesting that we should always provide "positive reinforcement contingent upon positive behavior." The extremists among them spent most of their free time and money at the teacher supply store buying stickers. If one of their students breathed or had a pulse, a sticker was given.

Where Does Love and Logic Stand on This Issue?
Listed below are some of my thoughts on the use of rewards with kids:

- The extremes on this issue ignore the complexity of human behavior.
- There are some very real risks associated with the use of rewards.
- When certain guidelines are followed, rewards can be very effective.
- Reinforcement theory is "built into" most of the Love and Logic techniques.
- With some very low-functioning kids, tangible rewards are helpful.

The Complexity of Human Behavior
Thank goodness none of us really knows how to completely control another! Children, as well as the many contexts within which they behave, are far too complex for any one theory to explain.

Risks Associated with the Use of Rewards
Listed below are some potential risks or "side effects" associated with the use of rewards:

• They can distract us from building sincere, positive relationships.

I've witnessed many well-meaning parents and educators who've become so focused on finding the right reward or consequence that they have forgotten the importance of building positive relationships with kids. There will never be enough rewards or consequences to get kids to behave if we are not first showing them how much we care. Rewards and consequences gain their true value from this relationship.

When children feel we don't care, rewards feel like bribes and consequences create resentment.

• Rewards often fail to address the underlying causes of behavior.

Most misbehavior is driven by unmet basic emotional or physical needs. While rewards and consequences may modify the observable behavior, the underlying problem may remain. As a result, behavior change is often temporary, or the child acts out in some other way in an attempt to get his/her needs met.

• Used unwisely, rewards can create dependency and entitlement.

Isn't it sad when we hear a child ask, "What do I get if I'm good?" Call me idealistic, but what I want for every child is the belief that the best way to feel good is to do something good.

Children who have been raised with frequent bribes in the form of "If you do _____, I will give you _____" become kids who live life with a "What's in it for me?" attitude.

• With strong-willed or oppositional kids, rewards create power struggles.

To understand this risk, let's take a look at the basic thinking pattern of the strong-willed or oppositional child:

Now that I know what you want ... I'll do the opposite.

Rewards send the following message to difficult kids:

I want you to do this so badly that I will give you something if you will do it.

When this message is received by the stubborn child, they do an immediate, albeit subconscious, cost-benefit analysis:

I wonder what would be more exciting? Would it be this reward they are offering? Would it be seeing their faces turn red if I misbehave by doing the opposite? Would it be fun to see them get frustrated when I whine about the smallness of this reward? Or ... would it be seeing their faces turn double red if I behave just long enough to get the reward, then act even worse after I get it?

Since doing the opposite of what we want (and seeing our faces turn red) is very rewarding to strong-willed kids, is it any surprise that rewards often make the problem worse in the long term?

• Focusing on rewards can be exhausting and stressful.

I've been truly saddened by the number of educators and parents I've seen who could no longer enjoy their kids because they're working so hard to keep track of points, checkmarks, tokens, stickers, or some other type of reward. Do kids pick up on this stress and act even worse? You bet!

Some Guidelines for the Effective Use of Rewards
Every effective drug has its side effects. Late last spring I was cursed with a quite nasty sinus infection. Fortunately, my doctor prescribed a common and very effective antibiotic medication. Unfortunately, I ignored his warnings to stay out of the sun while

taking this medication. As you may know, one side effect of anti-biotics is sensitivity to the sun. I learned a very valuable lesson from this.

Like antibiotics, rewards can be very effective if we "stay out of the sun" by following these guidelines:

- Build positive relationships and meet other underlying emotional needs.

Rewards can be very effective if the following needs are also being met:

Unconditional love, acceptance, and *empathy*
Physical and emotional safety
Friendships and a sense of group "belonging"
Healthy feeling of control
Limits from loving adults
Feelings of self-competence
Etc.

- Use *variable,* rather than *fixed,* reinforcement schedules.

What does this mean? Quite simply, using a *fixed* schedule of reinforcement means that we always provide rewards in a way that is predictable to the child. For example, when we say, "If you do _____, then I will give you _____," the child knows that he/she will be rewarded after doing what we say.

One of the common problems with fixed schedules is that children quickly learn how to work the "system" by behaving just long enough to get what they want. As a result, we run the risk of creating kids who believe that they only have to behave if they are given something in return.

Using a *variable* schedule of reinforcement simply means that we provide rewards in a way that is not predictable to the child.

Slot machines work this way—the players have no idea how many times they will need to pull the lever before they hit the jackpot. Because the payoff is unpredictable, many people can lose their fortunes thinking that the very next pull will be the big winner.

Decades of solid research shows that variable schedules of reinforcement are typically more effective than fixed schedules. Using a variable schedule means that we reward our kids when they are not expecting it. For example, let's imagine that a child has been particularly helpful. Applying a variable schedule, a parent might say: "I've noticed how polite and helpful you've been ... helping me with the laundry, dusting, and other things. It's really fun for me to show you how much I appreciate your help, so I bought you this CD you've been wanting. Here you go! Enjoy it."

Since this parent wants to avoid creating a demanding or manipulative kid, the child knows that there will be many times when he/she doesn't get a reward for helping.

• Don't fall into the trap of bribing, begging, or negotiating.

Most of us know at least one parent who constantly uses rewards in an attempt to bribe their kids into behaving. This bribing often evolves into begging as their children learn to negotiate for bigger and better rewards.

Parents who bribe create kids who learn
how to beg, negotiate, and argue.

At the grocery store one day I spotted a father who wasn't about to fall into this trap with his children. Trailing behind him, one of his kids whined, "What do we get if we're good?"

Without breaking stride, Dad smiled and answered, "A happy family."

• Use tangible rewards as infrequently as possible.

I feel very sad when I see kids—and adults—who can only feel good when they have a new toy. Does it seem like there's an epidemic of this thinking in our culture?

A very powerful way of creating healthier, more independent kids is by modeling the joy you experience when completing something challenging. When our kids see us feeling good about our accomplishments, they learn to feel good about their own ... even if they don't get a "reward" in return.

Reinforcement Theory Is Built Into Love and Logic

There's good news! With Love and Logic, you don't have to be an expert on behavior modification or reinforcement theory to very effectively use rewards. This happens automatically when you apply Love and Logic.

I'll never forget the teacher who proved this to me ... and herself. She'd been trained to use lots of stickers and pizza parties to reward positive behavior. She'd also been trained to deal with misbehavior by giving each of her students different-colored slips of paper. The system went something like this:

First misbehavior: change your color slip from green to brown.
Second misbehavior: change your color slip from brown to yellow.
Third misbehavior: change your color slip from yellow to red.

Kids with red slips had to stay in for recess.

Observing this teacher, I noticed that she had wonderful relationships with her students. She greeted them with a hug each morning, she was very warm, she was very well-organized, and she set fair and enforceable limits.

Rarely if ever did her students have to "change their colors" to red. As a result, this teacher was convinced that the stickers, pizza parties, and paper slips were doing the trick. Unfortunately, she was quite frazzled and tired at the end of each day. Keeping track of stickers, pizza parties, and paper slips is hard work.

Challenging her, I asked, "Do your kids behave so well because of the stickers, pizza parties, and paper slips ... or is it because you are a great teacher who has great relationships with her students?"

She answered, "Oh, it must be my reward system. That's what I was taught."

At the beginning of the next year, I asked her to experiment by doing without her system. With great fear and reluctance she agreed to give it a shot—mostly because she was getting so tired of keeping track of stickers, pizza parties, and paper slips—and she was going broke spending her *own* money on all of this.

It's the relationship that counts, not the rewards.

What did she discover? She realized that her students behaved for *her* instead of for stickers, pizza parties, and paper slips. She also realized that she had a lot more fun during each day ... and a lot more energy at the end of each day!

With Love and Logic you help your children
reap the true "rewards" in life ... responsibility,
self-worth, respect, and confidence.

© *2004 Charles Fay, Ph.D.*

The Road to Wisdom Is Paved with Mistakes
By Jim Fay
VOL. 20, No. 2

The long plane ride home was torture. Sleep, once I got home, was not going to be any easier. This was one of those days when the alarm went off two hours earlier because I was in the Eastern time zone. It was a day when I was on-stage for over five hours.

When I was not on stage I was trying to answer questions and solve problems for the participants. I spent the entire morning break doing so, and then went back to the stage. All but five minutes of my lunch hour were spent answering questions. I had to rush to the rest-room during that time. But if you can believe it, one anxious mom followed me there and was waiting when I walked out the door.

After the presentation was over, I spent a very long time trying to help participants, who brought one challenging question after another. To add to the difficulty, several of these people proved to have stronger needs to *tell* how impossible their lives were, than to *listen* to possible solutions. They had lots of "Yeah buts" and very little commitment to listen and focus on possible solutions.

Overall, if I could look at the day objectively, I might say that I did a lot of good for a lot of people. But as I traveled home, I couldn't think of one good outcome for the day. I was miserable. As my mom used to say, "My heart was in my throat." That, by the way, is how us plain folk, back during my early years, described the psychological term "depression."

I had worked hard that day. No, I had gone way over that line. I had worked far beyond my endurance. But that was not what made me depressed. What upset me was that I had not "walked the talk" during the last question-and-answer session. I had vio-lated much of what I stand for. And when that happens I have a hard time living with myself.

I could not think of one good thing I had done that day. All I could think of was how I had handled one very anxious mother. Each time I opened my mouth to give her an answer, and before I could finish my thought, she said "Yeah but" and started talking, and talking, and talking.

Now on a good day, one where I'm at the top of my game, I would have thought, "I need to do a better job of empathetic lis-tening before offering an answer." But no, I was far from the top of my game, blurting out, "Do you use that many words when you are dealing with your kids?" Needless to say, she became more anxious. Her words burst forth faster and my impatience grew.

Needless to say, I let this person down. Nothing was accomplished, except maybe to prove my potential for being a jerk. I had spent the day teaching about the importance of empathy, but displayed none when I had the chance to model it. There is nothing that makes me feel worse than to realize that I have not "walked my talk."

Relating this situation to Charles Fay, my son, he reminded me what a great learning opportunity this was for me. "Which of the basic principles of Love and Logic did you violate?" he asked. "You teach parents how important it is for them to take care of themselves by setting those loving limits. Parents who don't take care of themselves are unavailable to model healthy behavior."

Charles nailed it. His questions helped me remember how working past my endurance left me incapable of being the good example I needed to be. I needed to take a closer look at how I set limits on the use of my time and energy during a day of presentation. Setting these limits might leave a few people disappointed that they didn't get the extra perk of meeting with me personally. However, given the choice of this happening versus treating some people poorly and setting a bad example, it makes sense that I should model the very things I teach.

What would loving limits have looked like if I had been at the top of my game?

Love and Logic teaches that limits are set when we state how we intend to take care of ourselves, rather than what others are to do. This is called the "I will" message. This is how it might have sounded to the audience if I had done a better job:

During the morning I am going to take a five-minute break and then return to answer questions for the remainder of the morning break.

When lunch time comes I will be returning early so that I can be available for twenty minutes.

After the seminar is over I will have time to visit for twenty minutes and then will be leaving for the airport.

I am more than happy to answer well-thought-out, specific questions for those who can listen without interrupting. After

I respond to your question I would appreciate your letting me know if my answer is helpful and fits your question or concern.

Unfortunately, I did not do that, but fortunately I discovered the name of the mom who had to deal with me when I was at the bottom of my game. I couldn't live with myself until I called her to apologize and ask for a chance to show my better side. We had a great conversation, I provided some better advice. She was surprised and thankful. And I had a chance to redeem myself.

The best thing to come out of this was the great lesson I learned. I have to agree with Charles Fay when he says, *"The rode to wisdom is paved with mistakes."*

© *2004 Jim Fay*

The Impact of Anxiety on Academic Achievement: Why Too Many Kids Are Learning Far Too Little
By Charles Fay, Ph.D.
Vol. 20, No. 2

As the weather warmed ... and this school year came to a close ... I began to ponder how our society and schools are currently approaching student achievement.

As I did, I reflected back on the number of parents and teachers I'd met this year who said the same thing:

We've tried everything! Nothing seems to motivate this kid to learn!

Ouch! I was also struck by the following:

• Over the past three decades, research has provided massive amounts of information regarding how to most effectively teach reading, writing, arithmetic, and other essential skills.

- From this research, highly sophisticated curricula have been developed.
- Teachers are far better trained, and engage in far more in-service training, than ever before.
- The government is holding educators and schools to higher and higher standards of accountability.
- Increasing pressure is being placed on teachers to teach, parents to enforce homework completion, and students to learn.
- *We continue to see an epidemic of capable kids who do poorly and get turned-off to school and learning.*

Why are we failing to reach so many capable children when we have more sophisticated tools and training than ever? The causes are many. One hint might lie in the famous research of Robert Yerkes and John Dodson in 1908. Their basic results are shown in the graph below:

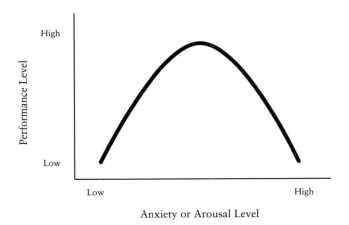

Anxiety or Arousal Level

There are very few "laws" or absolute truths in psychology. Nevertheless, research has so consistently supported this relationship between anxiety and performance that it is commonly referred to as the "Yerkes-Dodson Law."

Anyone who's ever taken a test ... or given a speech ... knows how "brain-dead" anxiety can make us. As soon as a moderate to severe threat is perceived, the brain triggers a "soup" of stress hormones, which are flooded into the body. In essence, the body and brain prepare for battle.

The psychological and cognitive consequences of this "fight-or-flight" are well known:

• Increased irritability and decreased frustration tolerance.
• Difficulty sustaining attention and remembering details.
• Difficulty following directions.
• Narrowing of perception (inability to see the "big picture").
• Inability to think abstractly.
• Difficulty understanding the connections between related details or facts.
• Perceptions and emotions are governed more by memories of prior threatening experiences than what is occurring in the here and now.

The negative effects of anxiety on academic performance become even more profound ... and frightening ... as tasks become more difficult. As the following graph shows, the effects of anxiety on children struggling with subjects they find difficult spell doom for the learning process:

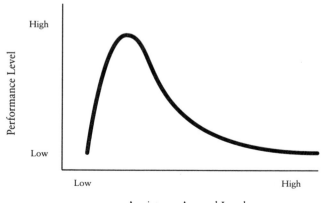

Anxiety or Arousal Level

Is it possible that, in all of our well-meaning attempts to increase academic achievement in our schools and homes, we are creating a climate in which kids are at-risk for experiencing the psychological and cognitive consequences of fight-or-flight ... on a chronic basis? And is it possible that all of this anxiety has its most negative effects on the very children who we are attempting to help the most?

Listed below are some common practices used to motivate kids to do their schoolwork at school and their homework at home. How might these affect *your* anxiety level?

- Lectures about the importance of doing your work, getting good grades, and how tough your life is going to be if you don't.
- Reminders of the potential consequences of getting poor grades.
- Being expected to learn material that your brain is not yet mature enough to process.
- Being expected to learn too much material, too quickly, with too few opportunities for repetition.
- Being expected to learn a large number of facts without enough opportunities to link these facts with previously learned concepts and real-life examples.
- Homework that requires skills that have not yet been taught at school.
- Having well-meaning teachers and parents who are so stressed about your learning that they are unable to convey genuine warmth, patience, and enthusiasm.
- Knowing that your parents ... and possibly your teachers ... are going to be really mad if you do poorly.

It's extremely tempting to fall into the trap of using these anxiety-elevating practices when government mandates for higher standards and educational accountability are placing us all in fight-or-flight. In essence, the following process seems to be unfolding between the federal government, state governments, school districts, educators, students, and parents:

The government tells school districts,
"Do a better job educating our nation's
youth ... or else."

↓

School districts experience fight-or-flight
and say to educators, "Do a better
job ... or else. "

↓

Educators experience fight-or-flight
and put more pressure on kids to learn,
and on parents to make their kids do
their homework.

↓

Kids experience fight-or-flight and
learn less and less

Given these current trends, what can educators and parents do to foster academic achievement without falling into the trap of pushing kids into fight-or-flight? Very generally, the key involves understanding that human beings learn best when they feel safe and anxiety is low. How is this achieved?

Positive Teacher–Student and Parent–Child Relationships
There exists nothing more powerfully motivating than relationships. When kids fall in love with their teachers, it's almost impossible to stop them from learning. When kids experience a sense of unconditional love from their parents, they are free to take the risks required to learn.

Anxiety over academic achievement stems largely from fears over losing love or respect if mistakes are made.

Quite simply, positive relationships create an environment where anxiety is low enough for kids to try challenging tasks, make mistakes, and learn from them.

Isn't it ironic ... and very sad ... that some parents and educators rant, rave, and ruin these relationships in an attempt to make kids do their schoolwork and get good grades?

Fortunately, there are many very wise teachers who know that their students are more likely to perform and learn if they are greeted at the door each morning with a smile. Thankfully, there are also many wonderful parents who understand that it's far more important to hug their kids than their kids' homework folders.

These highly successful educators and parents know that it's absolutely critical that children know the following:

The important adults in my life value learning and achievement, but they value me even more than my grades!

If I don't study, my life will probably be pretty hard ... but my parents will still love me and my teachers will still like me.

What would happen to the academic achievement and climate of our homes and schools if we simply changed the words we used with kids over schoolwork and homework issues? What would happen if we replaced the language in the first column below with the language in the second?

Get to work.	*How can I help?*
Why aren't you working?	*I'm going to like you regardless of the type of grade you earn in my class.*
This is important. It's going to be on the statewide test next week.	*This is a really amazing fact!*
These grades are unacceptable! You're grounded!	*How sad. I will love you regardless of how happy or sad you make your own life.*
You can forget about driving with those grades!	*How sad. I'd love to see you be able to drive ... but I'd hate to start getting you addicted to a lifestyle you might not be able to afford when you are older. You may drive when I see that you are preparing yourself for a lifestyle that can afford driving.*
Don't tell me you are stupid! It's not true.	*You say that you are stupid? Aren't you glad that I don't believe that?*
Just try this. It's easy.	*This might be a bit tough, but I'll like you even if it is!*

Obviously, the art and science of raising student achievement is far more complicated than simply developing positive relationships and keeping anxiety under control. Nevertheless, will any of the highly sophisticated techniques we know serve any good if youngsters are not lovingly connected with their parents and teachers?

The answer to this question is a clear *No!*

Maybe it's time to stop focusing so much on techniques and start focusing a bit more on kids. What do *you* think?

© 2004 Charles Fay, Ph.D.

Five Gifts for Your Children
By Foster W. Cline, M.D.
VOL. 20, NO. 2

As another Father's Day passed I reflected on my life and what kind of a father I was. What could I have done differently? What can I pass on to today's dads? Here are my thoughts for you. Read this article carefully, and hopefully when you're my age you can look back with few or no regrets.

I'm sixty-four. I've got grown kids and nearly grown grandkids. And if I could, I would change some things. I'd give my kids more important gifts, because it is always more fulfilling to give than to receive, and I would have given more of them. Especially on Father's Day. I'd make it memorable if I had to do it over again. I'd concentrate on five gifts.

Time

Money? No problem, we can always make more of it. But time? The pile of time always diminishes. Yeah, I spent time with the kids, but I could have spent more. I guess I didn't realize how precious those few weekends were. Basically, there's about a nine-year period during which father time is so precious. The kids only want to be with you, do things with you, and they're fun, to boot.

During later teen years, they pal with their buds. It's over then. But at about five or six through thirteen or fourteen ... *Wow!* Those are years that fathers can revel in! Only about seven years or 370 Saturdays or so ... *Woosh* ... they're gone. I wish there had been more camping weekends. More fishing time. More time doing things that didn't really cost a plug nickel, but things that they and I now see as priceless.

Doing

I admit it. I spent too much time with 'em watching stuff. I wish that for every movie and game we saw together, I had built a model with the boys. They don't remember squat about what we watched together. But they remember sailing our wooden boat on the lake, and the kites, and ... well heck ... they remember all the stuff we did together. Even hauling rocks and clearing land and shoveling horse droppings. But they don't remember much about movies and games. I'm kinda sorry we didn't make some really bodacious kites.

Virtues

How well did I model the virtues? I've been reading biographies of great men lately. Most say that their fathers were the most influential person in their lives. They extol the virtues of their dads. They say that their dads were honest, upstanding, fair, caring, strong, trustworthy, and reverent. Where would I stand when my kids rated me on those virtues? Virtues seem to wiggle into more importance as I grow older. I look back at the times I lost my temper, complained about the little stuff, and became low-grade demanding when it wasn't really necessary. I'm not real happy about those times.

Sharing

Did I share my dreams? Literally? Maybe not enough. Why the heck didn't I take those kids to work more often? They would have had fun sitting in on some of my consultations, and the staff would have loved to have had 'em there. Dads probably ought to take a kid to work at least four times a year. And reminiscing. I could sure have done more of that. My wife has fond memories of Minnesota family tales that her dad spun. I recorded a lot of those stories, but did I tell enough? I think my kids could have helped me more with those recordings. I could have involved 'em more. Shared more.

Encouragement

Winfield remembers when I marched when he practiced the baritone. Robin remembers when I was ecstatic about her art and riding. Kids need the "go for it" message. I was good at that. Encouragement isn't exhortation. It's not looking at what they could do better, but being enthusiastic about what they have done. Then they take care of the "doing it better" part. It's a little paradoxical. You ask the kids with enthusiasm about what they're doing and how they did it, and they do more and better. But you tell 'em to do more and better, they tend to stop.

Time, Doing, Virtues, Sharing, Encouragement. Just five little cheap but priceless gifts for Father's Day.

Good luck.

© *2004 Foster W. Cline, M.D.*

Picking Fights and Losing Battles
By Jim Fay
VOL. 20, No. 3

Are some kids born stubborn, or do they become that way as a result of the way they are raised? Well, the answer is yes. Some children, as a condition of inborn temperament, are less cooperative and more prone to resist being told what to do. And some kids, as a result of how they are raised, become more and more defiant and stubborn as they grow older.

We all know, or have heard about, those youngsters who are always so cooperative and anxious to please that they will do anything without complaint or foot-dragging regardless of how their parents talk to them. It is indeed rare to find more than one of these in a family. This child is the dream of most parents and teachers. If all kids were like this, there would be no need for this article.

The question for this article is, "Is there a way we can get better cooperation from our kids regardless of how strong-willed they are born?" The answer is yes. There is a way. A small change in the way we talk can result in much better cooperation, fewer fights, fewer temper tantrums, fewer needs for disciplinary action, less hate, and more loving relationships. Great bosses and leaders rely on what we are about to talk about. Great teachers use this technique every day.

Don't Set Yourself Up to Lose

Let's work backwards on this. We will study a situation in which a teacher creates a minor disaster in her classroom. Her attempts to control a situation result in a "blowout" by the student, creating a need for other professionals to be involved. Then we will look at how this could have been avoided in the first place. Once we have done this, we will take a look at the use of this technique in our own homes with our own children.

TEACHER: (speaking from across the room) "Jessie, why are you moving your chair? You don't need to do that. Move it back where it was!"

JESSIE: "Brittany is going to help me."

TEACHER: "You don't need her help. Now move your chair back where it was!"

JESSIE: "But I need help on this."

TEACHER: "Move that chair, or you're going to get sent to the recovery room."

JESSIE: "I don't have to. You can't tell me what to do. You're not my mother!"

At this point the situation deteriorated. Jessie was ordered to leave the room. She refused, and was threatened with disciplinary action. Hearing this, she ran screaming out of the room and other professionals were drawn into the situation.

A "Nobody Loses" Approach

Here is another approach to the very same situation. No battle line is drawn. Regardless of how the child reacts, she is actually obeying the adult's request. Both the dignity of the adult and the dignity of the child can be maintained. Disciplinary action to help Jessie learn the wisdom of cooperating with the teacher can be provided at a later time if necessary.

TEACHER: (walking up the student and whispering) "Jessie. I need you to move your chair back. Would you consider doing that for me? Thank you." (The word "consider" takes away any threat and eliminates the opportunity for Jessie to be defiant.)

JESSIE: "But I want Brittany to help me."

TEACHER: (still whispering) "I'm sure that's true, and I'd like you to consider moving."

JESSIE: "No. I don't have to."

TEACHER: (still whispering) "Thanks for considering it. Do you really think that it's wise to refuse when I ask in a nice way? Personally I don't think that's a wise decision. We'll talk about that later." (The teacher walks away and Jessie remains where she is provided she does not create a disturbance.)

Since Jessie was not ordered to move, she has already complied with the teacher's request. She was not told to move, only to consider moving. Nobody has lost a battle at this point. The other students are not aware of the problem and the teacher's authority has not been challenged in front of the group. Jessie's teacher now has the time to muster her forces and figure out how to deal with Jessie's lack of cooperation. If discipline is necessary it can be done in private.

Applying This Technique to Parenting

How many parents do you know who set themselves up for the same kind of battles by barking orders that may not be enforceable at the time? This can lead to deadly results. Children who recognize that they can defy their parents become increasingly insecure and prone to test limits. Each time a parental request can be ignored or defied, the authority of the parent is reduced in the eyes of the children. It does not take long before these kids think, "I don't have to do anything my parent says."

It is important to remember that Love and Logic parents are not permissive. Even though they treat their children with dignity and seldom bark orders, they expect that their wishes and requests will be honored. Their children believe in that old saying, "Your wish is my command."

Children who live in Love and Logic homes have learned through experience that everybody wins when they are cooperative. Now, have these kids ever tested authority? Sure they have. How else did they learn that defiance doesn't pay?

Just like the teacher in the second scenario, parents can set themselves up to be winners in the arena of authority figure by using some of the following "Thinking-Word Requests" instead of "Fight-Word Demands":

FIGHTING-WORD DEMAND:	"Take out the trash, and do it now!"
THINKING-WORD REQUEST:	"I'd appreciate your taking out the trash before bedtime. Thanks."
FIGHTING-WORD DEMAND:	"Don't you talk to me that way! You go to your room!"
THINKING-WORD REQUEST:	"Would you mind taking those words to your room? Thank you."
FIGHTING-WORD DEMAND:	"You come here right now!"
THINKING-WORD REQUEST:	"Hey, Pal. Would you mind coming here? Thank you."

FIGHTING-WORD DEMAND:	"Go help your little sister. Do it now. I mean it!"
THINKING-WORD REQUEST:	"Would you mind helping your sister now? I'd appreciate it."

Some readers might consider these "Thinking-Word Requests" as showing no authority at all. In fact, some readers might even say, "What a wimpy way to talk. How is any authority maintained when you speak so nicely to kids?" My answer is, "Don't be so quick to judge."

Let's take one of these examples and follow it through to show how kids can learn that it is always best to comply when parents ask in a nice way:

MOM:	"Would you mind taking those words to your room? Thank you."
SON:	"No! I don't have to."
MOM:	"Did I ask in a nice way?"
SON:	"I suppose so. So what? I'm not leaving!"
MOM:	"Not wise, son. I could learn a lot from this."

Mom walks off and allows her son to temporarily believe that he has won the battle. However, he will learn later about the foolishness of his decision.

The following day he asks his mom to take him across town to his soccer game and discovers the results of being uncooperative:

SON:	"Mom, will you take me to my game? Mrs. James can't drive today?"
MOM:	"I don't know. Did you ask in a nice way?"
SON:	"Sure. What's this all about?"
MOM:	"Yesterday I learned from you that asking in a nice way doesn't get the job done. Remember that little episode when I asked, in a nice way, for you to go to your room? What did you teach me at that time?"

SON: "I don't know."

MOM: "You taught me that asking in a nice way doesn't mean all that much. I'd appreciate your giving that some thought. And some day when I feel better about your level of cooperation, I'll be glad to help out."

This brave mom did this expecting her son to start begging, complaining, grumbling, and laying on the guilt. Of course, he did! Our kids don't complain when we let them treat us like doormats.

And, you ask, "Did she give in and drive him to his game after hearing his begging and complaining?" Did she ask, "Now, have you learned your lesson?" Absolutely not! His angry behavior proved to her that she needed to provide this important lesson for her son.

Think about it. Do kids learn best from hearing about consequences? Or do they learn best from experiencing them?

When President Theodore Roosevelt said, "Speak softly, but carry a big stick," he was not only talking to world leaders, but also talking to us as parents and to our need to be loving authority figures for our children.

© 2004 Jim Fay

The Problem with Entitlement
By Foster W. Cline, M.D.
VOL. 20, NO. 3

Thirty years ago, Jim Fay and I used to teach that homes had to operate the way the "real world" operated and urged parents to prepare America's children for that real world.

Lots of things have changed in thirty years, and now we teach parents to raise their children with Love and Logic so they can grow up, become leaders, and *change* the way the "real world" operates.

Thirty years ago, an "American hero" was a soldier who fought courageously, overcoming great odds. Today, an "American hero" is a soldier who handles being a prisoner. Thirty years ago, people admired great actors and athletes but no one confused them with heroes. Thirty years ago, a lot of things were different.

Parents felt safe disciplining their children in public. The government did not concern itself with where and how a child sat in the family car. On lakes, fourteen-year-olds could take small outboard boats out to catch bass. Folks could buy sweet, unpasteurized, fresh apple cider at October Fests. Special ed classrooms could sell popcorn and fudge as a fundraiser for kids with special needs without needing to have a government commercial kitchen license. People had to give consideration to where they built homes, 'cause they would be paying their own money if they were flooded out or the homes were blown away. People could actually legally ride bikes without helmets in all states. This list could go on for many pages. Needless to say, our country has changed in many ways both good and bad.

Citizens of a nation respond exactly as do children in a home. The way parents handle a home and the way government handles the citizens have a profound effect on character development. Citizens, or children, who are protected entirely, not only lose their freedom completely, but also become progressively disabled, less self-sufficient, and far less responsible.

The greater the protection, obviously, the less an individual has a need to cope. I watch with both concern and sorrow when parents get more concerned about how fair a teacher is than about whether their kids are listening and learning in class. Many citizens revel in the role of victim and all the joys of plaintiff largess. I see parents rushing to buy their children another car or bicycle that was left unlocked, protecting their children from any possibility of painful consequences from poor choices. They unconsciously take as their model a government that rushes for the third or fourth time to rebuild homes in obvious disaster areas. I find that parents are paying for dental costs of children who don't brush, and piano lessons for children who don't practice, thus copying a government that pays billions for the health care of Americans who suffer from health problems that they create for themselves.

How early does entitlement start? It may begin with the pacifier, for I recently saw a young mother, who, oftentimes when her infant cried, was Joanne-on-the-spot with a pacifier. She insistently popped it in her toddler's mouth, even though the child was coping fine without it. The expectation that someone else should fix it—which feeds a feeling of national entitlement—has swept our country in the past thirty years like an out-of-control wildfire. Citizens insist that the government provide medical care, insurance, free lunches, and free medicine, rather than providing effective help for those who suffer in situations not of their own making.

Where does it start?

Perhaps it all starts with how a child's small fall is handled during toddlerhood, in which a parent's natural reaction varies all the way from, "Oh, Honey, how awful, can Mommy fix it?" to "Oops, I know that hurt, but look how well you're handling it!"

Across America I see adolescents who are quick to tell their parents what they "need" to do for them. "You need to buy me ..."; "You need to take me ..."; "You need to get me a lawyer ..."; "You need to ..." What do you think the odds are that these teens are being raised by adults who are saying the same kinds of things to government, thus casting their votes to any person who can offer them the most.

Unfortunately, few people recognize the hypocrisy of a national news magazine in which a cover story attempts to teach parents the importance of "saying no" while the same magazine's editorials encourage parents to vote for the politician who guarantees the largest government handouts.

But there is great hope. Even as some citizens become progressively less responsible and less able to pay for their own care or retirements, and even as they become more dependent on government giving, while raising older children who are unable to cope and who live at home—children who must rely on parental largess—I nevertheless take heart. For all across America, I see thousands of trained instructors teaching thousands of parents the joy of Love and Logic and the advantages of raising children who are self-sufficient; children who are allowed to make mistakes while regarding every mistake as a learning experience; children who are raised by parents who are empathetic without being overly rescuing; children who naturally become responsible, respectful, and fun to be around. There is a new day a-dawning when a new national guidance will take place with Love and Logic leadership as these children grow to maturity.

© 2004 Foster W. Cline, M.D.

The Highs and Lows of Entitlement

By Jim Fay

Vol. 20, No. 4

"So, Sara, what's happening in your life that brings you into counseling with me?"

"It's my parents. They're clueless! They are so lame! All they can do is bitch and moan about my credit cards and phone bills. They are *so* living in the past. They don't get it. There's lots more important things than grades. And they don't have a clue about what kids need. My dad bought me this stupid four-door car. He knows I was supposed to get a convertible. Nobody drives a heap like that to school."

"When your dad called to set up these sessions, he told me that money is really tight and that if things don't change, he will have to consider bankruptcy. Given the situation, do you feel any guilt about the amount of money you spend?"

"Of course not! I didn't ask to be born into this stupid family. Besides, that's what parents are supposed to do. They're supposed to buy great stuff for their kids."

I don't know who to feel sorry for: Sara, her parents, or the future of America. As outrageous as Sara seems, we all know kids like her. Sara and her counselor are real people. Sara is suffering from the belief of entitlement. I actually feel somewhat sorry for Sara.

Once she started to believe that it is her birthright to have everything she wants as soon as she wants it, she was doomed. She will never have enough to satisfy her. Her happiness will not be based upon what she can attain through effort, but will depend upon how others serve or provide for her. She will enter the adult world expecting far too much from others and far too little from herself.

Sara's parents tore up their parent license early in her life. By treating her like an honored guest in the home, they became product and service providers instead of parents. As the years went by, they stripped her of the need to act responsibly. As you can tell, she has become more and more dependent on her parents while becoming less and less appreciative of what they provide.

As Sara enters the adult world, what her parents once provided will become society's responsibility. And as you can guess, that will never be enough to satisfy her. Entitled people see themselves as victims. Once this sets in, all unhappiness and all disappointments are the fault of others.

Sara's parents, in their efforts to create a perfect life for their child, failed to teach her that living in a democracy requires personal restraints regarding personal behavior. Her discussion with the counselor indicates that she has no ability to see how her personal behavior impacts others, both in her home and in society.

Unfortunately, parents who try to teach personal responsibility are consistently faced with the fact that it is not reinforced in other parts of their children's lives. What is reinforced is a belief in limitless entitlement.

Many kids arrive at college with wealth that they have not earned. They actually have no idea how to attain or maintain their lifestyle other than demanding it from their parents. They have lots of money to spend, but no idea how to earn it. In other words, they don't have a clue that the money they spend comes from someone else's hard work, sacrifices, and responsibility. They have pockets full of credit cards without the knowledge about how to use them responsibly.

The authors of Love and Logic have major concerns about the rapid growth of entitlement in our young people and its threat to the American way of life. As we study this problem we have become aware of the beliefs that entitled people harbor. I like to call them the "Highs and Lows of Entitlement." As you read you will become aware that they are all debilitating beliefs:

HIGH: High need for goods and services.
LOW: Low pressure to succeed or to hold down jobs.

HIGH: High amount of time to party.
LOW: Low amount of time to devote to effort toward accomplishment.

HIGH: High expectations of others.
LOW: Low ambition.

HIGH: High resentment for those who would require them to achieve through study and effort.
LOW: Low appreciation for the opportunity for an education.

HIGH: High demand for entertainment and excitement.
LOW: Low awareness of the sacrifices made by their parents.

HIGH: High willingness to defy society's traditional rules and values.
LOW: Low respect for adults and leaders.

HIGH: High inclination to find substitute "highs" such as alcohol and drugs.
LOW: Low respect for society's traditional rules.

These problems and beliefs don't start when kids leave high school. The foundation for these beliefs is created in early life. Actually, this problem is not started by kids, but by parents who fail to set reasonable limits for behavior. It is normal for kids to want what they see advertised. However, many parents don't do a good job of helping their kids distinguish between a "want" and a "need." Young children don't naturally place limits on themselves. This is the parent's job.

I often hear parents say: "I don't know what's wrong with kids. They just want all this stuff." These parents act like they don't have a say in the matter. This is not unlike the parents who can't understand that the reason their kids watch too much television is because they allow it. These are the parents who have torn up their parent license. It doesn't have to happen to you.

Faced with society's pressures and the fact that personal responsibility is not reinforced in many parts of our lives, parents need three things:

1. Parents need to hold tight to their belief that kids need to learn how to get what they want through effort and struggle.
2. Parents need skills for setting and enforcing limits and boundaries.
3. Parents need to surround themselves with like-thinking friends so that they don't have to listen to the mistaken beliefs of those who are busy creating entitled children.

Dr. Yates, president of Colorado State University, says, "Until we can find ways to create a responsible coalition that includes not only universities, but also the high schools, parents, and the leaders of our communities and our country, the culture of self-indulgence will be hard to overcome."

Your Kids Can Be the Fortunate Ones
Dr. Yates is right. However, we have seen many parents who are successful at helping their kids avoid the infliction of entitlement. Parents who study and use Love and Logic parenting techniques up the odds of raising kids who are not inflicted with entitlement:

• Fortunate, indeed, are the children whose parents are willing to let them struggle for, and earn, the goods and services they want.

- Fortunate, indeed, are the children whose parents subscribe to the "matching funds" approach. These parents help their child buy goods and services with money after the kids earn and save a portion of the cost.
- Fortunate, indeed, are the children whose parents expect their children to do their fair share of the work required to maintain a household.
- Fortunate, indeed, are the children whose parents set loving limits, give their children reasonable choices, and allow consequences of those choices to prepare them for the adult world.

Take an in-depth look at childhood entitlement in our new book *From Innocence to Entitlement*. In Love and Logic tradition, the book offers specific and practical techniques for parents to use in combating childhood entitlement.

© 2005 Jim Fay

Marriage: Love and Logic Isn't Just for Kids
By Foster and Hermie Cline
VOL. 20, NO. 4

I was asked to write a different sort of article to introduce you to a groundbreaking Love and Logic Press publication, *Marriage — Love and Logic*. For the first time, Love and Logic will be focusing on a book about adult relationships.

Like all of the Love and Logic materials, this publication will provide practical tools that you can immediately implement to improve life in your home. But this time my wife, Hermie, and I are focusing on enhancing couples' relationships.

Marriage is packed with the attitudes, beliefs, tools, and techniques that have been beneficial for the hundreds of couples whom we have worked with in groups and on retreats. They are tools and concepts that have worked equally well for us during our forty-five years of marriage, living with the seven children who at one time or another graced our lives.

Love and Logic has always taught that the important things are learned by the great Es: Example, Experience, and Empathy. To provide you with examples, a DVD will be provided with the book. On it, a lovely couple wrestles with the *Love and Logic Concepts and Experiences* that we provide in the book. The dozen or so *Love and Logic Experiences* themselves are structured exercises of exploration and communication that lead to a deeper understanding and appreciation of your relationship.

Rather than go on and on talking about the book, we'll give you an overview of the content. Eighteen communication tools are described. Using the *Love and Logic Report Card* in the cover of the book, you will rate yourself and your spouse on how well you use those tools.

Love and Logic Percent Desire is one of the tools we describe. Percent Desire is a way to quickly reach compromises. Don't use Percent Desire when compromising on "bombshell" issues. Bombshell issues require a lot of thoughtful discussion and don't lend themselves well to quick and effective compromising. However, the Percent Desire method might be very effective when two new movies have come to town. You want to see one, but your spouse is inclined toward the other. Percent Desire works best on the issues that lead to the following silly discussion:

HUSBAND: "As long as we are going to see a movie, I'm willing to see *Guts, Guns, and Blood.*"

WIFE: "You've wanted to see that for a long time ..."

HUSBAND: "Yeah, but I know you've wanted to see *Quilting Ladies Play Bridge.*"

WIFE: "Well, how much do you want to see *Guts and Guns?*"

HUSBAND: "Oh, I'd like to see it, but maybe not as much as you'd like to see *Quilting Ladies ...*"

Let's assume that this couple only has one car, or they don't want to see their movie of choice alone and there is not a third choice that they both really want to see. In such cases, Percent Desire settles the problem quickly—generally to each one's satisfaction.

To use the Percent Desire method, you both choose a percentage number between 1 and 100 that represents the level of your desire for your choice. You tell one another your number, and then go happily (!) to the choice of the person with the highest number.

The less trust a couple has, the more difficult it will be to use this method. Some couples banter back and forth saying things like, "You tell me your number first" or "Write it down, so you can't change it!" That's not trusting.

Percent Desire is best used on *nonthreatening* issues: "I know you would like us to both stay home, but I would really like for us to go out. Let's decide it with the Percent Desire method."

This is obviously *not* for bombshell issues like, "Okay, you come up with a percentage about how much you want that very expensive car and I'll come up with a percentage of how much I *don't* want you to have the car!"

Trusting occurs when you have fully accepted the idea that when your partner wins, you win. Similarly, when you win, your partner wins. Percent Desire maximizes your win quotas within the relationship. The more often you win together, the more your relationship grows. Some decisions are not either/or. For instance, in the movie example, the couple might see a film they'd both like to watch. Or, if both movies were showing at the same theater, they could split up and watch their own choice separately.

Percent Desire is just a simple shortcut for averting issues over which we wonder, "Well, how much does my partner really want this or that?"

Now let's look at a simple *Love and Logic Experience* you can have some fun with, a little exercise that ensures communication clarity. It is a "sit down and talk it over" experience. No writing. Play with it when the two of you are riding in the car or at the dinner table. (Actually, it might be fun to play it with your kids.) One is the interviewee, and one is the interviewer.

The person being interviewed picks a couple of the following statements and fills in the blanks:

"The thing I like most about Christmas is _____."
"The thing I like most about our family is _____."
"My greatest accomplishment is _____."
"One thing in my life I wish I had done is _____."
"The thing I like best about you is _____."
"One hope I have for the future is _____."

Now the one doing the interview asks, "Do you mean ____ ?" The person being interviewed must respond three times with a "yes" to move on to the next statement. For instance:

HUSBAND: "The one thing I wish I had done in my life is hang glide."
WIFE: "Do you mean you have a sense of adventure?"
HUSBAND: "Yes."
WIFE: "Do you mean you like flying in general?"
HUSBAND: "No."
WIFE: "Do you mean that you blame me a little bit for discouraging you from doing it?"
HUSBAND: "No."
WIFE: "Do you mean that if I set something like that up for you to experience you'd be happier than a toe stomping grapes?"
HUSBAND: "Yes."
WIFE: "Do you mean you would rather go hang gliding than horseback riding in Colorado this summer?"
HUSBAND: "Yes."

End of exercise. And end of this article! Stay tuned!

Accountability, 42, 43, 142, 195
  empathy/consequences and, 92
  for educators/schools, 193
  for kids, 67, 90, 117–18, 122, 123, 135, 136, 138, 139, 149
  See also Responsibility
Achievement, 210, 215
  anxiety and, 192–98
  effort/struggle and, 118, 124, 166
  high, 103, 104, 105
  increasing, 195, 196, 198
  pride in, 52–53, 188, 197
  problems with, 103, 104
  standards for, 123
ADD *See* Attention Deficit Disorder
Addiction, 13
  computer game, 179–82
  depression and, 180
ADHD *See* Attention Deficit Hyperactive Disorder
Adolescence, 120
  challenges of, 93, 109
  follies of, 129–31
AdvancedAcademics.com, 65
Agreements, broken, 146–50
Alanon, 76
Alcohol, 100, 109, 116, 179, 210
  decisions about, 8, 9, 22, 29
Allowances, 4–5, 169–70, 171, 172
Amotivational syndrome, 94
Anger, 4, 31, 33, 34, 36, 40, 65, 75, 82, 100, 109, 137, 153, 156, 164, 172, 205
  avoiding, 39, 101, 142
  dealing with, 44
  feeling, 72, 81, 138, 141
  lying and, 141
Anti-reward activists, 182
Anxiety, 85, 115, 196
  academic achievement and, 192–98
  rumors and, 86
Anything Goes Parent, 29
Arguing, 4–5, 35, 44, 109, 141, 179
At-risk children, 60, 100, 195
Attachment, modeling and, 152
Attention, difficulties with, 137, 194

Attention Deficit Disorder (ADD), 13, 38, 163
Attention Deficit Hyperactive Disorder (ADHD), 47
Attitude
  improvement in, 104, 142
  problems with, 104, 105
Authority, 203, 204
  challenging, 110, 202, 203
  independent thinking and, 121
  listening to, 78–82

Bad guys, 125, 135, 136
Bandura, Albert, 152, 153
"Basic German Shepherd," responding to, 15
Battles, 71, 200–205
Bedroom time, 32, 33
Bedtimes, handling, 71
Begging, 187, 205
Behavior, 53, 152, 166, 182
  changes in, 114, 184
  copying, 153
  improving, 35, 60
  modeling, 162, 191
  problems with, 41, 108, 126–27, 143, 162
  responsible, 103
  rewards and, 153–54
  standards for, 123, 209
Behavior modification, 188
Belonging, sense of, 186
Bipolar problems, 93, 163
Birthday parties, toxic, 82–84
Biting, dealing with, 41
Blaming, 44, 92, 116, 123, 128, 139, 167, 215
Body language, 62, 76, 159, 160, 161
Bombshell issues, 213, 214
Bonding, 6, 21, 61, 153
Boredom, dealing with, 45–50
Boundaries, 161, 211
Brain drains, 34
Bribes, rewards and, 184, 187
Brott, Boris, 28
Bulldozer approach, 8

Bummer, 16, 44, 91, 92, 152
Bumps and bruises, handling, 110, 158–62, 207

"Can do" message, 106
"Can't" versus "won't", 106
Cause and effect, 120
Causes, treating, 34–37
Certified nursing assistants (CNAs), 157
Character, 84, 124, 148
  building, 41, 50–56
  government and, 206
  perfect image and, 124
  trust and, 53
  valuing, 41–45
Chemical imbalances, 109
Choices, 3–4, 79, 166
  consequences and, 68, 89, 100, 118–19
  elderly parents and, 156, 157
  giving, 6, 7, 17, 18, 36, 39, 50, 119–21
  learning from, 20, 92
  making, 10, 16, 76, 77, 78, 89, 101
  poor, 8, 10, 22, 23, 29–30, 91–92, 116, 118–21, 143
  real-life, 22, 90, 120, 182
  small, 30, 37, 73, 74, 119
  wise, 9, 120, 121, 141, 202, 212
Chores, 45, 103, 154, 167
  doing, 47, 48, 49, 151, 165, 170, 182
  easygoing kids and, 101
  extra, 102, 142
  finding fun in, 145–46
  money for, 172
CNAs See Certified nursing assistants
Codependent situations, 76
Cognitive deficits, 94
Communication, 53, 94, 214
  tools for, 213
  verbal/nonverbal, 111
Competence, experiencing, 101, 120
Compliance, 80, 88, 210
Computer games, addiction to, 179–82
"Concrete Operations" thinking, 11

Conditioning, 70–71, 81, 82
Conflicts, 42, 43, 135
Connections, 60, 194
Conscience, foundation for, 51, 52
Consequences, 116, 130
  allowing for, 10, 78, 121, 212
  choices and, 42, 68, 89, 100, 118–19
  delayed, 19, 141
  delivering, 17, 23, 35, 44, 92, 136–37, 139, 141, 162, 176, 184
  depression and, 109
  effective, 17, 66, 175–76
  empathy and, 36, 92, 101, 163
  experiencing, 42, 43, 174, 205
  humor and, 173–76
  learning from, 20, 89, 92, 170
  misbehavior and, 42, 43
  natural, 44, 75, 121
  negative, 30, 52
  pets and, 19–22
  psychological/cognitive, 194, 195
  real-world, 42, 90, 120, 182
  rescinding, 126, 136
  warnings and, 87, 88, 89
Consistency, 61, 126
Consultant Parent, 29
Control, 86, 119, 174
  external, 14–15, 46, 182
  healthy, 35, 36, 186
  impulse, 143
  loss of, 118, 182
  self-, 52, 163, 169
  sharing, 73, 74, 101
Cooperation, 61, 103, 104, 105, 141, 200, 203, 204–5
  gaining, 201
  lack of, 202
Coping, 113, 115, 121, 163, 207
  inability for, 207
  modeling, 110, 176
  need for, 206
  problems with, 106, 107
  rescuing and, 65, 114
  skills for, 63–66
  tragedies and, 85–87
Copying, 62, 152, 153, 154, 206
Counseling, 128, 162–65, 208

Courage, 66, 67
Creativity, self-discipline and, 143–46

Damaging messages, 83
Defensiveness, 44, 98
Defiance, 110, 202, 203, 210
Delayed gratification, 47, 143
Demands, 31, 33, 199
Denial, power of, 179
Dependency, 184, 207
Dependent learners, 68–74
Depression, 190
    addiction and, 180
    causes of, 109, 110
    coping with, 163
    physical/biological basis of, 111
    treating, 108–13
Depression and Related Affective
        Disorders Association, 113
Developmental problems, 104, 105,
        106, 163, 182
Developmental steps/stages, 27
Dignity, 202, 203
Directional remediation, 107
Discipline, 30, 81, 82, 106, 124,
        137, 138
    building, 50–56
    disagreeing about, 126, 136
    exploration and, 145
    external, 51
    good relationships and, 38
    private, 202
    public, 206
    threatening, 201–2
Discomfort, 118, 123, 166
Disobedience, 16, 17, 58
Distractions, 16–17
Divorced parents, 135, 136, 137, 138
Dodson, John, 193
Doing, 200
    getting and, 47–48
    gift of, 199
    happiness and, 49
    watching and, 145
Drill Sergeant Parent, 29, 174
Drugs, 15, 78, 100, 110, 148, 179,
        210
    decisions about, 8, 9, 22, 29

denial of, 164
experimenting with, 75, 76, 97,
        129, 130
resisting, 97, 99

Early childhood, creativity during,
        145–46
Easygoing kids, 99–102
Eating disorders, 100
Eating patterns, 110
Education, 65, 76, 117, 210
Effort, 118, 123, 124, 166, 211
Elderly parents, 155–58
Emotional problems, lying and, 143
Emotions, 39, 159, 161
    governing, 194
    honesty with, 85
    responsibility for, 111
Empathy, 49, 86, 143, 213
    consequences and, 36, 92, 101, 163
    expressing, 7, 19, 44, 61, 73, 92,
        111–12, 141, 162, 172
    importance of, 191
    learning and, 53, 170
    unconditional, 186
Encouragement, 162, 200
Energy drains, repaying, 142
Enforceable statements, 16, 73,
        74, 203
Entertainment, 46, 47, 48, 210
Entitlement, problems with, 83, 166,
        184, 205–12
Excuses, 58, 63, 122, 135
Expectations, 50, 52, 112, 167
    high, 106, 210
Experiences, 53, 213
Experimenting, 71, 152, 153
Exploration, 144, 145
Extended care facility, 157

Facts, giving, 85–86
Fear, creating, 85
"Fighting-word" demands, 203–4
Fight-or-flight, 194, 195, 196
Fights, picking, 200–205
Financial responsibility, gift of,
        169–73
Firmness, 39, 40, 41, 153

Follies of youth, 129–31
Follow-through, 126
"Formal Operations" thinking, 11
Four Steps to Responsibility, 101, 170
Friends, importance of, 84
Frustration, 4, 33, 34, 57, 65, 81,
    82, 153
  decreased tolerance for, 194
  experiencing, 41, 168
  lying and, 141
  self-concept and, 165

Getting, doing and, 47–48
Gifts, for children, 198–200
"Go for it" message, 200
Good guys, 135, 143
Good persons versus happy persons,
    135–39
Government, dependence on, 207
Grandparents, 128, 151, 152, 154
  listening to, 79–80
  money management and, 171
Great Depression, re-creating in the
    home, 171
Gross motor developmental skills, 53
Guilt, 109, 156, 205, 208

Happiness, 209
  doing and, 49
  money and, 173
  responsibility for, 111, 166
  short-term/long-term, 136, 165–68
Happy persons versus good persons,
    135–39
Harnesses, 14–15
HDD See Honesty deficit disorder
Health, 114, 206
Helicopter Parent, 29
  "Turbo-Attack" model, 121–24
Helping, 86, 113–15, 152–53
Homework, 193, 195
Honesty, 77, 78, 85, 140, 142, 148, 199
Honesty deficit disorder (HDD),
    139–43
Honored guests, 117, 167, 209
"Hot button" issues, 129
"How sad," 197
Humor, consequences and, 173–76

"I love you" messages, 9
"I love you too much to argue," 5,
    44, 141
"I" messages, 17
"I'm not ready" indicators, 98–99
"I'm ready" indicator, 99
Inconvenience, 118, 166
  facing, 66–68, 123
Independence, 121
  building, 69, 73, 74, 188
Independent living facility, 155, 157
In-home care, 157
Interference, 57, 118
Internet, 29, 42, 165, 179
Intimidation, 122, 124
Irritability, 108, 109, 194
"I will" messages, 191–92

Joy, 49, 155, 188
Just say "no," 15, 82–84, 98

Keeping up with the Joneses, 82–84
Kid-referenced statements, 27

Late bloomers, 105
Leadership, preparing for, 120
Learning, 62, 113
  empathy and, 53
  observational, 153
  performance and, 197
Learning opportunities, 89–92, 170,
    191, 208
Learning problems, 47, 103, 104, 107
Lecturing, 50, 92, 99, 100, 141, 170
  avoiding, 101, 142
  spouses and, 127–28
Letter-reversal, 108
Licensed care facility, 155
Limits, 135
  enforcing, 61, 112, 139
  setting, 23, 31, 32, 36, 136, 153,
      182, 186, 191–92, 210–11, 212
  testing, 33, 87, 203
  undermining, 126
Listening, 60, 106, 111, 190, 191
  importance of, 58, 86
"Live and let live" rules, 76–77
Living alone, 156–57

Loners, thinkers/leaders and, 11
Love, 52, 152, 176
    communicating, 112–13
    need for, 35, 36, 186, 196
Love and Logic, 59, 173
    elderly parents and, 155–58
    using, 4, 19, 98, 104, 125, 127–28,
        143, 158, 162–63, 175, 182, 188
"Lucky Genetics Club," 99
Lying, 42, 139–43, 147, 148, 181

"Magic moment," 12
Manic-depressive problems, 93
Manipulation, 33, 61, 98, 125, 187
Marriage
    healthy, 128
    Love and Logic and, 212–15
"Matching funds" approach, 212
Maturity, childhood nonsense and, 105
Mental illness, 93, 111
Misbehavior, 45, 118, 135, 136, 139
    consequences and, 42, 43
    emotional/physical needs and, 184
    stopping, 35
Mistakes
    affordable, 102, 170
    consequences and, 42, 89
    making, 7, 42, 43, 101, 102, 208
    real-world, 90
    thinking about, 66, 130, 138
    wisdom and, 189–92
Modeling, 6–7, 45, 47, 85, 158, 171,
        176, 188, 191, 199
    attachment and, 152
    importance of, 128, 151, 153, 155,
        162
    potty training and, 154
Money management, 169–73, 198, 209
Morality, 123
Mornings, handling, 70–71, 93–94
Motivation, 94, 144, 151, 195
    self-, 52, 53, 146, 182
Motor output delay, 103, 107
Music, in utero, 27–28

National Institute of Mental Health, 113
National Mental Health Association,
    110

Needs, 35, 37
    wants and, 211
Negativity, 3, 108, 109
Neurological conditions, 104, 105,
    106, 142–43, 163
Newborn schedules, 12
"No problem," 91, 92, 115
"Nobody loses" approach, 202,
    203–5
Noticing, 37, 61, 62, 146, 153, 187

Obedience, 40, 41, 52, 202
One-liners, 5
Options, keeping them open, 87–89
Overprotection, 65, 97

Parenting, 99
    courses, 154
    fun of, 174
    instincts, 142–43
    styles of, 29–30, 38, 124, 125–28
Parties, 97–99, 168, 210
Passivity, 53, 104
Pediatricians, visiting, 158–59
Peer pressure, 100, 105
    resisting, 8–10, 23, 97–99
    writing about, 9–10
Percent Desire method, 213–14
Perfect image, 123, 124
Performance, 110, 124
    anxiety and, 193, 194, 197
Personal property issue, 149
Pets, consequences and, 19–22
Pixie Stix, 83, 84
Plans, 98, 99, 114, 181
Positive behavior, positive reinforce-
    ment and, 182
Potty training, 5–8, 150–55
Power, 40, 153
Power of attorney, 156
Power struggles, 8, 120, 184
Pressures, 193, 210, 211
    See also Peer pressure
Pride, gift of, 173
Problems, 45, 162
    handing back, 42, 48–49
    solving, 46, 111, 166, 174, 189
    source of, 92, 166

Promises, hearing, 57–58
Protectiveness, 42, 43, 115, 118, 123, 142, 206
Psychiatrists, 111, 165
Psychic space, 175
Psychologists, 112, 165

Quiet moments, 46, 49

Real world, 22–23, 42, 90, 101, 182
  experiencing, 205
  learning about, 44
Reasonable, 5, 24–25
Reasoning, 121, 141, 142
Rehabilitation facilities, 157
Reinforcement, 182, 188–89
  fixed/variable, 186–87
Relationships, 94
  building, 60, 184, 212
  positive, 59–62, 103, 104–5, 106, 196–98, 201
  problems with, 8, 105, 130, 137, 196
  rewards/consequences and, 184, 189
  teacher–student, 196–98
Reminders, 72, 101, 170, 195
  offering, 24, 69–70, 182
Requests, 57–58, 203
Rescuing, 64, 66, 82, 113–15, 125, 130, 139, 163
  avoiding, 121
  coping and, 65, 114
  life/health and, 114
  special needs children and, 114
  unfairness and, 67
  warranted, 114–115
Resentment, 16, 84, 89, 140, 156, 210
Resistance, 118, 124, 128, 200
  hating school and, 103
Respect, 61, 76, 78, 93, 120, 136, 148, 163, 165, 189, 208
  building, 36, 44, 52, 59, 61, 62, 121
  expectation for, 112
  low, 210
  words of, 31, 34

Responsibility, 18, 67, 76, 78, 84, 90, 93, 104, 111, 116, 135, 136, 148, 165, 170, 189, 208
  benefits of, 166
  building, 9, 19, 30, 41, 73, 209
  elderly parents and, 157
  long-term, 21
  losing, 207
  money and, 209
  parental, 149, 150
  personal, 209, 211
  resisting, 163
  sense of, 167
  teaching, 8–9, 20, 21, 92, 123–24
  valuing, 41–45
  worrying about, 74
  See also Accountability
Responsiveness, 4, 59, 81, 104, 165
Retraining process, 32, 58
Rewards, 153–54, 182–89
  bribes and, 184
  effective use of, 185–86
  risks of, 182–83
Right thing, doing, 43–44
Risks, 110, 121, 182–83
Routines, maintaining, 86
Rules
  breaking, 116
  compliance with, 88, 210
Rumors, anxiety and, 86

Sad voice, using, 36
Safety, 14, 15, 126
  feeling, 85–87, 112
  physical/emotional, 186
Saving, teaching about, 169–70, 172
Saying no, 15–18, 51, 87, 207
Schizophrenia, 93, 163
School
  hating, 103–8
  intimidating, 122
  talking about, 160–61
  unfairness at, 63–66
Self-centeredness, 32
Self-competence, 186

Self-concept, 31, 179
  damaged, 42, 43
  easygoing kids and, 100
  frustration and, 165
  good, 60, 62, 116
Self-discipline, 51, 52, 53
  creativity and, 143–46
Self-esteem, 30, 35, 37, 100, 101, 120
Self-image, 52, 107, 108
Self-indulgence, culture of, 211
Self-referenced statements, 27
Self-respect, 52, 53
Self-sufficiency, 206, 208
September 11th terrorist attacks, 85
Set up to lose, example of, 201–2
Sex, decisions about, 8, 9, 22, 29
Sharing, 25–27
  gift of, 199–200
Skills, 53, 63–66, 99, 176, 181,
    192, 195
  decision-making, 101
  leadership, 115
  learning, 3, 59
  survival, 22–23, 101
"Sky Rage," 65
Sleep, importance of, 93
Sleeping patterns, changes in, 110
Spanking, 18–19
Spare time, creativity with, 45
Special needs children, rescuing, 114
Speech patterns, 62
Spoiled brats, 30–34, 82
Standards, setting, 123
"Sticker commandos," 183
Strengths, 118
  communicating, 85, 86
  noticing, 37, 61, 62, 146, 153
Stress, 72, 109, 173, 185, 194, 195
  lowering, 140
Strong-willed kids, 38, 59, 61, 99
  cooperativeness from, 201
  power struggles with, 184
  rewards and, 185
  stress of, 128
  thinking patterns of, 184–85
Struggles, 101, 123, 124
  benefits of, 166, 211
  protecting from, 118, 168

Success, 76, 210
  effort and, 118
Suicide, 100, 110
Survival skills, real-world, 22–23, 101
Symptoms, treating, 34–37

Taking care of self, 75–76, 84, 87,
    162, 191
Task focus, 13, 53
Teachers
  pressures on, 193
  relationships with, 60
  successful, 197
  wrath toward, 167
Television, 46, 49, 53, 94, 127, 144,
    145, 168
  Attention Deficit Disorder and, 13
  conversation/thinking and, 14
  limiting, 13–14, 39, 211
  poor choices and, 29
Temper tantrums, 31, 51, 150, 170, 201
Temperament, inborn, 200
Therapy, 111, 112, 162–65, 181
Thinking, 27
  abstract, 194
  causal, 51, 52, 114
  independent, 121
  patterns, 184–85
"Thinking-word" requests, 203–4
Threats, 81, 99, 100, 128, 151, 194,
    201–2
  avoiding, 101
  responding with, 141
Time, 200
  gift of, 198–99
Tone of voice, 31, 36, 76, 86, 159,
    160, 161, 162
Tough times, facing, 65, 115, 162,
    173–74
Traditions, 130, 158
Tragedies, coping with, 85–87
Trophy kids, 116–19, 124
Trust, 51, 52, 59, 75, 98, 140, 141,
    147
  character and, 53

"Uh, Oh Song," 32–33, 34
Undermining, 126, 127, 128, 135, 139

Unfairness, 108, 140
    coping with, 63–66, 115, 141
Unhappiness, 166–67, 168, 209

Values, 41–45, 61, 77, 84, 210
"Velcro child," 159
Victimhood, 65, 123, 166–67
    encouraging, 64, 206
    entitlement and, 209
Violence, decisions about, 8, 22
Virtues, 200
    gift of, 199

Wake/sleep cycle, reversed, 93–94
Wants, needs and, 211
Warnings, 22–23, 99, 100
    avoiding, 40, 87–89
Watching, doing and, 145
"What's Your Plan?" strategy, 98
Whining, 40, 144, 170, 187
Wisdom, 101, 189–92
Withdrawal, 108, 109
"Won't" versus "can't," 106
Working conditions, negotiating,
        141–42, 143

Yates, Albert: on culture of self-indul-
        gence, 211
"Yeah buts," 190
Yerkes, Robert, 193
Yerkes-Dodson Law, 193
"You are strong" messages, 9
"You are weak" messages, 9
"You can't cope" messages, 106

Sign up for the *Love and Logic Journal* for yourself, a friend, or your child's teacher.

The *Love and Logic Journal* gives you the positive reinforcement you need.

Our quarterly publication is a great way for parents and teachers to connect with Jim Fay, Charles Fay, Ph.D., and Foster W. Cline, M.D., on a regular basis. In each issue of the *Journal* you will discover the very latest techniques from Jim, Charles, and Foster, presented in an insightful and humorous style. You'll also find exciting articles by guest writers from across the country who are developing creative and innovative ways to use Love and Logic in the home and at school.

Return this order form with your payment TODAY.

Yes! I would enjoy more practical solutions from Jim Fay, Charles Fay, Ph.D., Foster W. Cline, M.D., and other Love and Logic supporters. Please sign me up for a 1-year subscription to the *Love and Logic Journal* at $18. I understand that along with my subscription I may select one free audio valued at $13.95. (Colorado residents, please add 3% [54¢] sales tax to subscription price.)

❏ Check enclosed
❏ Please charge my ❏ VISA ❏ MasterCard ❏ Discover Card

— — —   — — — —   — — — —   — — — —

Card Expiration Date ____/____ Verification # _____
(found on back of card)

Signature _____

Take advantage of this special BONUS DISCOUNT!

As a *Journal* subscriber you will receive a bonus coupon good for a one-time 10% discount on a variety of Love and Logic books, audios, and videos. You will find this coupon inside the complimentary *Journal* issue you will receive with your free audio. (10% discount excludes package offers, *Becoming a Love and Logic Parent®* program and companion workbooks, *Early Childhood Parenting Made Fun!* program and companion workbooks, *Discipline with Love and Logic* teacher training course, and 9 *Essential Skills for the Love and Logic Classroom®* training program and companion workbooks.)

NAME _____

DAYTIME PHONE (_____) _____

ADDRESS _____

CITY _____ STATE _____ ZIP _____

EMAIL ADDRESS _____

Call Customer Service at 800-338-4065 for information on your free audio.